Editor-in-Chief and Founder:
Lyndon H. LaRouche, Jr.
Editorial Board: *Lyndon H. LaRouche, Jr. , Helga Zepp-LaRouche, Robert Ingraham, Tony Papert, Gerald Rose, Dennis Small, Jeffrey Steinberg, William Wertz*
Co-Editors: *Robert Ingraham, Tony Papert*
Managing Editor: *Nancy Spannaus*
Technology: *Marsha Freeman*
Books: *Katherine Notley*
Ebooks: *Richard Burden*
Graphics: *Alan Yue*
Photos: *Stuart Lewis*
Circulation Manager: *Stanley Ezrol*

INTELLIGENCE DIRECTORS
Counterintelligence: *Jeffrey Steinberg, Michele Steinberg*
Economics: *John Hoefle, Marcia Merry Baker, Paul Gallagher*
History: *Anton Chaitkin*
Ibero-America: *Dennis Small*
Russia and Eastern Europe: *Rachel Douglas*
United States: *Debra Freeman*

INTERNATIONAL BUREAUS
Bogotá: *Miriam Redondo*
Berlin: *Rainer Apel*
Copenhagen: *Tom Gillesberg*
Houston: *Harley Schlanger*
Lima: *Sara Madueño*
Melbourne: *Robert Barwick*
Mexico City: *Gerardo Castilleja Chávez*
New Delhi: *Ramtanu Maitra*
Paris: *Christine Bierre*
Stockholm: *Ulf Sandmark*
United Nations, N.Y.C.: *Leni Rubinstein*
Washington, D.C.: *William Jones*
Wiesbaden: *Göran Haglund*

ON THE WEB
e-mail: eirns@larouchepub.com
www.larouchepub.com
www.executiveintelligencereview.com
www.larouchepub.com/eiw
Webmaster: *John Sigerson*
Assistant Webmaster: *George Hollis*
Editor, Arabic-language edition: *Hussein Askary*

EIR (ISSN 0273-6314) *is published weekly
(50 issues), by EIR News Service, Inc.,
P.O. Box 17390, Washington, D.C. 20041-0390.
(703) 777-9451*

European Headquarters: E.I.R. GmbH, Postfach
Bahnstrasse 9a, D-65205, Wiesbaden, Germany
Tel: 49-611-73650
Homepage: http://www.eirna.com
e-mail: eirna@eirna.com
Director: Georg Neudecker

Montreal, Canada: 514-461-1557

Denmark: EIR - Danmark, Sankt Knuds Vej 11,
basement left, DK-1903 Frederiksberg, Denmark.
Tel.: +45 35 43 60 40, Fax: +45 35 43 87 57. e-mail:
eirdk@hotmail.com.

Mexico City: EIR, Sor Juana Inés de la Cruz 242-2
Col. Agricultura C.P. 11360
Delegación M. Hidalgo, México D.F.
Tel. (5525) 5318-2301
eirmexico@gmail.com

Canada Post Publication Sales Agreement
#40683579

Postmaster: Send all address changes to *EIR*, P.O.
Box 17390, Washington, D.C. 20041-0390.

Signed articles in *EIR* represent the views of the
authors, and not necessarily those of the Editorial
Board.

Shut Down Wall Street This Week; No More Suicides!

Shut Down Wall Street This Week; No More Suicides!

Dec. 13—With so-called "junk debt" markets plunging, and experts warning of a "riot in the Wall Street casino" this week if the Federal Reserve raises rates, *EIR* Founding Editor Lyndon LaRouche today made a very strong proposal; indeed, a demand on the elected representatives and citizens of the United States.

"Close in on this and shut this Wall Street casino down, this week." LaRouche said, "Remember what is the *effect on the people* of this kind of crash. We cannot have more suicides, or any more of what happened in Italy last week."

Italy is in an uproar since an Italian citizen committed suicide after an insolvent bank expropriated all his savings in an outrageous "bail-in" procedure, which also expropriated many others across four failing banks. This infamous "Cyprus-style" procedure has been repeatedly used in Europe as banks collapse.

And more expropriations are coming: "People have been being murdered by their banking systems," as LaRouche put it.

In the United States the sudden "junk debt collapse" is only a harbinger of a Wall Street collapse worse than 2008, with worse impacts on human livelihoods on a global scale.

LaRouche added:

We cannot allow it to continue. You have worthless accounts, of so-called debt "assets" which are in collapse, and they're being used to kill people's income, their employment, potentially their food supply, and even to kill them. If you don't shut down these Wall Street "funds," now, you will see what has just happened in Italy, on a grand scale.

I mean it is an "edge of death" situation, if we don't shut down those pretended assets. Close down the Wall Street system. Bankrupt it as Franklin Roosevelt did during his Presidency.

Then, countries have to create national credit for productivity and employment, again as Roosevelt did.

It is Barack Obama who has blocked restoration of the Glass-Steagall Act, which is the key to bankrupting Wall Street and allowing productive credit to take effect on the economy.

The same Obama has brought in the "Paris climate agreement," so-called, which —*if it were to be carried out*—would reduce the economy's ability to support human life by 80-90% in the next 35 years.

"This is a bold human genocide if allowed to occur," LaRouche said. We can't allow it to occur.

"That means closing out Wall Street—and that includes Donald Trump—and getting Obama out. Good people in both political parties can agree, to move the responsible authorities in Congress to get these objectives done."

creative commons

A poster in one of the Italian towns where bank policies resulted in what's called "austerity suicides." It reads: "I thought I could fly, But my bank has clipped my wings. A business without credit is a business without a future."

EIR Contents

www.larouchepub.com Volume 42, Number 50, December 18, 2015

Cover This Week

The New York Stock Exchange at Wall Street

Creative Commons

Shut Down Wall Street This Week; No More Suicides!

This issue is the last *EIR* edition for 2015. Our next issue will be dated Jan. 1, 2016.

Brunelleschi in Manhattan

Here are excerpts from Lyndon LaRouche's Dialogue with the Manhattan Project on Saturday, December 12, 2015. A video of the event is available.

Dennis Speed: My name is Dennis Speed and on behalf of the LaRouche Political Action Committee, I'd like to welcome you to today's meeting. I believe this is the 27th meeting, but I want to say this:

Lyn, everybody today, has or has access at least, on the table in the back, to an *Executive Intelligence Review* magazine simply entitled "Brunelleschi." Now, our Manhattan Project is over the next week going to go into a new phase, and the music will be leading that. And that musical process, which will reach a certain level, particularly over next Friday, next Saturday, and Sunday, has already been started here today, with what Diane just did, especially her last reference to the question of the Solar System being inside one's head.

So Lyn, I'd like you to do something today which I'm requesting, which is an opening statement which takes us past the noise of the Barack Obama apologizers of this week, such as Donald Trump and others; and puts us on a different plane so we can consider this concept you've put forward about the unity of the nation, and the need for people, good people, be they Republican, Democrat, Independent, or other, to come together and accomplish what you've outlined can be done, which is the immediate removal of Barack Obama from office, and the immediate defeat of Wall Street, but by use of these methods that you had uniquely pioneered. And the Brunelleschi *EIR* just brought this to my mind. So I know I don't usually do that, but I'd like to ask you for an opening statement, and then we go to Q&A.

Brunelleschi's Rope Song

Lyndon LaRouche: Yes, I think the important thing for us to consider is what was actually accomplished with Nicholas of Cusa, but prior to Nicholas of Cusa, and what preceded that. And therefore, once you place your ideas of judgment in that category, suddenly you find yourself in sort of a happy state of mind; that you are sure that you're on the right ground; you realize that there's creativity. And you go through the Brunelleschi series entirely. And Brunelleschi is a very complex question for people to deal with, who are particularly *ingénues*, because they don't understand it.

creative commons/Sailko

The Santo Spirito church in Florence, designed by Brunelleschi not long before his death.

But in the time of Brunelleschi's leadership, he was *really a master* in this area. And that was something on which the foundation of modern civilization has depended, on the great achievements of Brunelleschi. And everything else followed from that.

But that's a whole story in itself. It's something,—we've just gone through a choral practice, and the idea of a choral practice, which you've just been doing again this afternoon, and what we do in society in general, are one and the same thing. There has to be a harmonic agreement which is not simply singing notes one after the other, but going with the idea that everything you've done up to a certain point, requires that you make an innovation to the next note; and then to make another one, again, an innovation to the next note. And that's exactly what Brunelleschi did. And the best illustration, is he composed or constructed a harmonic chorus, which was *totally beautiful music, itself,* absolutely beautiful in his composition, in this small area that he occupied for this subject-matter. And this thing set a standard for all wise people, to look up and see something beautiful.

Speed: Thank you, Lyn. He's referring to the Pazzi Chapel, I believe.

And I'd like to have us go to the first question, which is here.

Q: My name is J— W—. And I love that we're doing notes, and starting on notes, because my gosh, we've got some crazy notes going on in politics—like Trump and Hillary Clinton. So who, as a bipartisan coalition, would you see helpful to bringing some harmony in our country?

LaRouche: I think, the point is, why not go from the beginning, from Brunelleschi; And Brunelleschi was actually the founder of modern science, in many ways. He did everything, everything imaginable. The list of his accomplishments is immense. But his building of the Florence Cathedral, that particular construction, which anyone can see these days still,—this was a magical development, and it reflects his mind.

And the small occasion that he struck there, in that little temple kind of place, the Pazzi Chapel, a musical temple, is one of the most beautiful little things ever produced, and it sets the standards for all kinds of beautiful things, in poetry, music, and so forth, in general. And so he is one of the great geniuses who brought the future of mankind into possibility.

Q: [follow-up] In our bipartisan coalition that we would like to see happen in this country, do you see any particular individual whom we could anchor in on, and get some better music notation?

LaRouche: Well, in terms of my own experience, I search for these kinds of opportunities. And by that I mean, when I'm dealing with something, I don't like to do something I think is either shabby or dull. And therefore I think my impulses always are to get some element of beauty,—that is,— but beauty in the true sense, not beauty as some kind of construction. But when you just try to do the things that you think are the next things which should happen, which is what Brunelleschi did in his practice, if you go back into his history. We're doing this now, it's a big story.

But what he did, he set up whole systems. Like this idea of a rope,—if you take a rope and you pull a rope across the stream, and the rope has a flexibility in it. So the people who are walking across this rope, from one shore to the other,—and this one of the famous things of Brunelleschi. And his treatment of "yes, no; yes, no; yes, no," and so forth, was a typical part of his whole mental life. And he used this to induce people how to trust a rope system, as you walk as a human being across the rope from one shore to the next. And people were doing that. In Italy up to the recent time, this thing of the Rope Song ("Funiculi, Funicula") was a very common feature of the culture.

In other words, imagine you had two points across a river. You create a flexible structure of the type Brunelleschi himself made, developed, designed. And you walk across the thing, and you find that the rope dances. And in order to cross the river, you must dance, in a sense, across the rope. When you move on the rope, you change the direction of the rope, in terms of the walking; and you can think that backwards and forwards, and that's what the Italian standard was. And people up to the present, or recent time at least, remembered that song, about the dancing rope.

Because there are two points; you have one rope, with a slack in it, and you're going to use the slack as in a piece of music. So you step on the rope; now when you make the next step, you're going to a different point in the crossing of the rope. The effect is that the rope effectively dances, according to your steps of moving in one direction or the other. And this is typical of the concept of construction which Brunelleschi represented.

And up to recent times, people used to sing that song, the Rope Song, created by Brunelleschi. And this is one of the principal methods of demonstration of

The Tibetan funicular bridge in Claviere, Italy.

what he was trying to convey, to the minds of the people who were actually using that rope to cross a stream. And that's still a valid thing today, as even in my youth, or a little bit later, I was part,—you know, you would sit there and you were thinking, you were thinking about the dancing rope; but just imagining that you were walking from one step to the next in either direction, in terms of passing over that rope. And this idea created an idea in the mind of the people who were walking across this rope, from the point of departure to point of arrival. And this was an Italian theme, which dominated everything since Brunelleschi, up to a recent time, of the dancing rope.

Trump and Hillary Clinton

Q: [follow-up] How can we apply that to our bipartisan issue here, politically, with Trump and Hillary Clinton, and how can we....?

LaRouche: Very easily, just do it. The way to do it, is you go backwards. What you do, is you construct the experiment. Now, Brunelleschi did a lot of that. Everything that he did, including the whole development of the chapel that he created,—he did everything that way.

And so therefore, everything worked.

He built the whole structure of the tower based on creating a shell which had a space, a shell within a shell. And I and my wife Helga walked up that system, inside the shell. You have also in the Italian music records, the same thing; you have the choral presentation there. It was all there. It's still all there.

The problem is, you don't have a population today which has that sense of experience. And the best thing we can do, is to take Brunelleschi's old work, including the tower that he built; and that will give you an education, because you are forced to follow certain ropes, with values. And you realize that your music is the way the rope moves when you walk across it. And by designing that thing as what you can do in music, is the same thing. You can change the character of the rope, and that will change the tune of the walking of the rope, across the stream.

Q: [follow-up] Sounds good to me. Thank you very much! [applause]

Q: Okay Mr. LaRouche, it's a pleasure to actually be here, actually meet with you, and not to mention that singer-songwriter Mariah Carey will perform here at the Beacon Theater tonight. And so it's a pretty wonderful experience, you know, to learn more of the notes that take you back to high school, with the music notes that we just pronounced here.

Basically, my name is C— J—, and I'm actually an owner of a law firm. And so basically my primary concern is, in regard to Barack Obama, our President, who is supposedly in violation of the 25th Amendment. So I wanted to know, basically in order to require more of my students, and to teach more of my law students more with regards to the 25th Amendment; and as far as the Congress, who, as far as not producing any functioning or producing any reins, on his behalf as far as not contributing to him violating the 25th Amendment; and as far as them not *per se* doing anything in regards of him moving in directions away from Constitution, or violating the Constitution. What do you think on that?

LaRouche: When I looked as to Obama's function, it was at the beginning of his career. And I looked quickly at what he was up to. I had a large core group which was gathered around me on this business, and I launched the identification of what Obama meant, and before the end of the week, I had Obama's number. And my justness on his number was never lessened; I was right from the beginning. *He only became worse.*

And if we want to have a civilization, you must remove any leadership which corresponds to that of Obama. He is identical with the idea of a Satanic mentality. I think there are certain Roman emperors, Nero for example, who would fit exactly what Obama represents today.

Q: [follow-up] Definitely. So do you think that he and the British Crown are affiliated with each other, as far as coinciding with each other?

LaRouche: They're identical. The Roman legacy, that is the ancient Roman legacy, is still the foundation of the British System.

Q: [follow-up] Definitely.
LaRouche: It's evil.

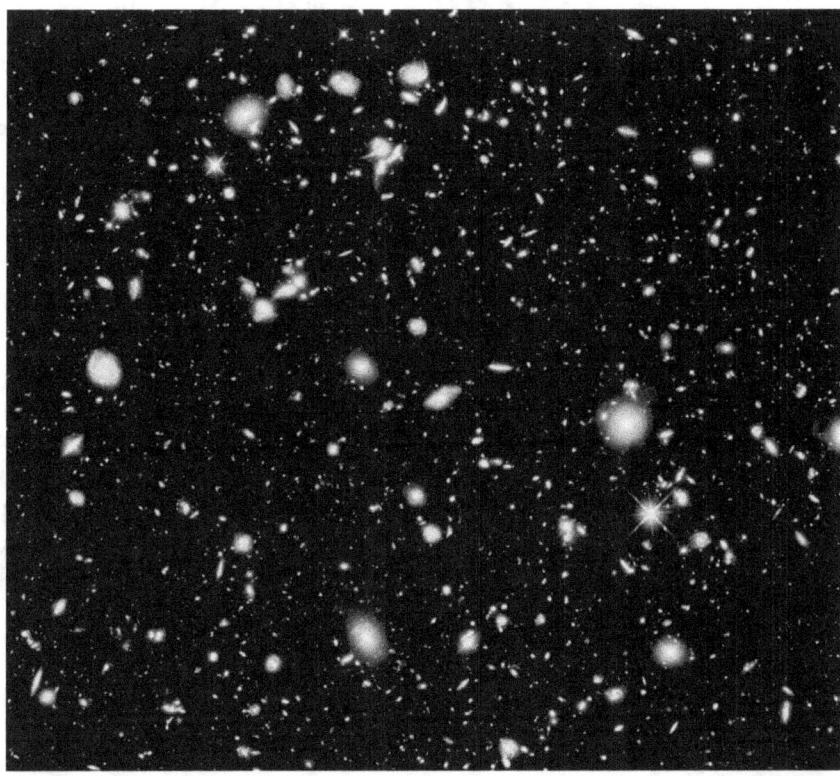

A Hubble telescope image of a constellation of galaxies.

Man is Not Self-Contained

Q: [follow-up] So, what do you think as far as Congress is concerned? And what is their functional role because of his violating the 25th Amendment to the Constitution?

LaRouche: It's obvious. Mankind has to create. Mankind is not something that is going to be fixed. This is stupid, the way it's done. And the ignorance with which people approach the subject, by habit, by induced habit, is really very destructive.

Because mankind is not a self-determining creature. Mankind is a response to the potential of not only the Solar System, but the Galactic System. Now, here mankind is actually,—from our own experience, mankind has progressed in understanding itself by educating itself to get these ideas of physical principles, or what is the effect of physical principles, and to recognize that that is the natural tendency. And when you study the Galactic System as such,—and the Galactic System is a very large and varied system. It's an immense thing. We have very limited actual knowledge of the scope of that principle.

But what we find out, is that we can adduce the destiny of mankind from the standpoint of things like the Galactic System. But the Galactic System is only one part of a larger system, which is the whole system of the Solar System and beyond. And so therefore, mankind must come to an agreement with that objective. And you get that with Kepler. Kepler is a big change in the system, his accomplishments. Then you go to another layer, a higher layer of discovery. From Einstein, for example. Einstein is one of the greatest models for introducing the concept of what the human mind is properly directed to do.

And we have not explored this thing fully. We just know that mankind is not the stupidity of a single human being. No single human being, *per se*, is adequate to be a human being. Mankind must always be moving in a direction which goes to mastering challenges, as Einstein did in his time; to find a creative pathway to a higher level than mankind has ever known before.

So mankind is not *sui generis*. Mankind is not something which creates a Solar System *per se*, but rather mankind adapts to the opportunity of the Solar System and beyond; and mankind is not a self-contained creature. Mankind is a guided creature, guided by the heavenly powers, so to speak; those heavenly powers which are way beyond anything mankind had known before. *But* the crucial thing, if you follow that pathway of improvements, you are acting in *harmony* with mankind's destiny.

Q: [follow-up] I think it's well said. I very much appreciate it, Mr. LaRouche. Thank you.

Q: Hi, Mr. LaRouche, my name is C—. I've been looking into Brunelleschi ever since you mentioned the triad with Brunelleschi, Cusa, and Kepler. And one of the things that stood out for me when I was looking into the subject,—you know, with arches, an arch structure is not stable until you put in that last centerpiece, the keystone. And with domes that were built in that time, they needed the centering, and they were only stable when the keystone was put in place.

With Brunelleschi's dome, it never required any of that. It was self-standing throughout the entire process. And there was a contemporary during that time who described that, because he grew up watching Brunelleschi do this incredible thing, and he described it such that it was the catenary effect which allowed for every brick to be a keystone. I was wondering if you could maybe elaborate on that?

Impeach Obama

LaRouche: Simply, this is something which I'm very familiar with. I've spent a good deal of time particularly in Italy, when I was working in that area with some of the people, the Italians who were gifted Italians at that point; and with their whole system. And this is something which is natural.

But the point here always is that mankind is not a self-developing personality. Mankind has a destiny of improvement of man's powers, in terms that mankind is able to foresee the powers of mankind, to achieve effects which mankind would not otherwise be able to accomplish. This is something which goes to a higher level than what we think of as given facts or given kinds of facts.

Everything important about mankind can be reduced to the requirement that mankind *must* develop to a higher level of self-development. Mankind does not create self-development, but mankind tickles the potential of self-development. And that's what we call the discovery of creativity. And the best example of that, the simple case of that, is Einstein. Einstein did exactly what has to be done: To discover what the future is, to discover what mankind's options are, to realize nothing less than something better which you can understand in those terms. That's what Brunelleschi did. That's the

way it works, and that's the *only* way it really works satisfactorily.

In other words, mankind does not come out and say, "I'm a great genius." And walk out and say, "I'm a great genius." What does that mean? What's the standard by which you discover what this so-called alleged genius is? And you look at Einstein, and you look at his major series of developments, and you see the same thing. You'll see the same thing *earlier* in the work of Brunelleschi. It's all the same thing. It's the immortal conception of mankind, to always go to a higher level of creativity, not within the opinion of the existing mankind, but of a comprehension beyond, for man, beyond mankind's accessed knowledge, then.

It's the future, the creation of the future to a higher level. This does not come from man itself. It comes from the destiny of mankind, as a discovering agency, which reaches a higher level than mankind has ever reached before.

Q: Hi Mr. LaRouche, I'm R— from Bergen County, New Jersey. I apologize if I am a little bit disorganized today. But it was last night that I came across Jeff Steinberg's excellent presentation [in the Friday, Dec. 11 Webcast], and an article from LPAC brought my attention to a new development in the Congress called H. Res. 198, submitted by Mr. Yoho. And I would like to get your thoughts on this, but to me this is an extremely interesting development, where the purpose of the resolution is to define impeachable high crimes and misdemeanors.

Without reading a lot of it, it says that: "The absence of impeachment standards creates an appearance that [as read] impeachment is a partisan exercise, which undermines its legitimacy and deters its use; and whereas the impeachment power in the House of Representatives is a cornerstone safeguard against Presidential tyranny…" etc.

And then they go through and define the Presidential impeachable offenses, and it's pretty amazing when you read down the list, because there's nothing in the list that hasn't been violated numerous times by the last two Presidents. For example, initiating war without Congressional approval, killing American citizens, failing to superintend subordinates guilty of chronic Constitutional abuses—the list goes on and on and on. You can read through it and see there are probably hundreds of instances in which all of these conditions have been violated by the last two Presidents.

But it raised to me the question of why has Congress held back? I mean, it looks to me as if there is some kind of emerging consensus in some sense coming into existence, which is reflected by this H. Res. 198.

But I went back and re-read the Preamble to the Constitution, and I asked myself: Has Congress actually defended any of these conditions in the Preamble to the Constitution? "In order to form a more perfect Union." Has Congress helped to form a more perfect union? I don't think so. "Establish justice?" Have they been defending justice? Not with regard to Wall Street, for example. "Ensure domestic tranquility"—we're not seeing a heck of a lot of domestic tranquility these days. "Provide for the common defense?" are they doing that with the rise of ISIS? "Promoting the General Welfare?" Well, they sure as heck have *not* done that. "Securing the blessings of liberty to ourselves and our posterity?"

Bottom line is, it looks like Congress over the last 15 years has done nothing to defend the Preamble to the Constitution.

So my question to you is, according to the Constitution, does the Congress have the obligation to meet the requirements of the Preamble, or is that an option for them?

Beyond that, it looks like, if these diverse elements come into the existence in the Congress, as reflected by Yoho's House resolution, it seems that LPAC, in that case, plays an essential, very important and historic role in being a catalyst to bring those elements together, to force these issues to be confronted.

The Example of Einstein

LaRouche: Let's take the case of Thomas Jefferson. Thomas Jefferson was the force of evil working against the foundation of the United States. And since that time, there have been a great number of Presidents of the United States, who have, like Jefferson, maintained a commitment to this evil, or relative evil at least. And this has been the dominant feature among the Presidencies of the United States; and by the local states in particular. The Southern states in general are hopelessly degenerate on these questions.

And the very best of our Presidential system of recent vintage, is a number of Presidents who typify the effort to bring about—. But then you find out that the President of the United States,—while Franklin Roosevelt seemed to be a great genius, but when the new election came [in 1944], he was replaced by the FBI, the development of the FBI. Once the FBI was set into

motion, the corruption of the United States was consistently, but irregularly, going in a direction *downward, downward, downward, downward.*

Now therefore, in this situation we have to operate on the basis of understanding a universal principle which was already grafted, in at least its raw essence, by the founding of the United States. And what you have from our great first leadership of this thing, which led to bringing in the Washington institution as a President,—from that point on, was being savaged in one degree or another, ever since.

Now, if we understand what the original principle was, and understand the measures by which you can test the principle, that's the only solution that we have. We have to go back to the original Constitution of Alexander Hamilton, in particular. Hamilton had the most precise insight into what these principles meant. Like the four first measures on economics. And if you look at his four cases, and apply that, that would be sufficient to demonstrate what the inconsistency is of most practices since that time from more or less evil, or just stupidity.

So the point is, if we understand that principle, we have a guide to clean up this mess. Now, of course, Obama we have to get rid of entirely; the Bushes—you have to burn the Bushes. God says burn the Bushes! Get these Bushes burned out and *clean it up.* And we need to have a Presidency which finally says, no, *we are not going to go one step further in this kind of monstrous behavior, which we have been doing as a nation up and down in various ways, during the best of times.*

We've come to a point of crisis, and it's a crisis which deals with the question of the United States and other nations of the planet as a whole. We have to bring about a new condition among nations. We're working on a fight on this for China; we're trying to rebuild India's prospects; we're looking at efforts in Japan; we're looking at new canal systems, which are major canal systems, and all kinds of things. We're also working on recognizing that mankind is not a creature limited to the Earth as such—that we also have to respond to what are the implications of the Earth existing within this system, including the aquatic system, like the Galactic System. And these are factors which mankind must take into account.

The most efficient example is that of Einstein. Now Einstein was absolutely unique, among all the people of his time, absolutely unique. It was the time in the Twentieth Century, when the Twentieth Century was going through a process of early disintegration and degeneration; and it's been going more and more deep into degeneration ever since.

So we have to stop the process of degeneration which has been given to us by recent authority, since Franklin Roosevelt's death. And we have to *exactly* put in a new conception of mankind, which is in knowledgeable accord with what mankind should be. It's not a perfect one, but it's a knowledgeably sound one, which will lead, hopefully, to more and more improvements of man's role inside the Solar System, inside the Galactic System, and beyond. We have to discover the mystery of what the purpose of the existence of mankind is in the universe, and follow that pathway.

FDR Library
Real Presidential leadership: FDR at the dedication of the Boulder Dam on Sept. 30, 1935.

The U.S. Presidency

Q: Hi Mr. LaRouche. I would like to ask you if Sen. Bernie Sanders, the Senator from Vermont, becomes the Democratic Party nominee for President, would you be able to support him? Would you be able to work together with him, if he becomes President?

He is saying that we must bring back Glass-Steagall, and that we must divide the wealth of the nation evenly. He's against the rich corporations getting away with the tax loopholes and not paying any taxes at all, or very little taxes. And Senator Sanders is for the working-class families and for the middle class. So I'm just wondering, do you think he would make a good President? Would you be able to work together with him and advise him?

LaRouche: Absolutely not! Absolutely not. He's a fraud.

We've got another candidate up there, who is much more capable, and much more intelligent, who is also hesitating on the edge on this thing. But the problem is that we don't have any prospect, a functional prospect, to create a new Presidency. Now we could create that. And I'm aware of means by which we could create that, with the existing institutions of government that are the foundations of our Constitution. And I think O'Malley would be a more likely candidate than anyone else on the screen right now.

There are other people—you know, I've supported Ronald Reagan; I was actually a part of his team, for a time. And then they got me out of there, because they wanted to get me out; they wanted the Bushes in there. And since then we've been living in the Bushes. Which means that everybody who's been functioning since Ronald Reagan was shot,—he did survive—but he was shot by an associate of the Bush family. And therefore everything has been backed down.

I was sent in to become, together with a great Einstein tradition figure, with the two of us—Teller. Teller and I were actually collaborators in this thing. And we had been collaborating ever since, for most of the decade.

And so we went with this, and we came up with a good program. But what happened with Reagan, when Reagan got shot, is that the Bush family interest took over, heavily, and since that time we have not had a good Presidency in any sense. We had Bill Clinton, who was the only approximation of that, and he had problems of getting his own government into shape. He never did get a full government, because his Vice President was a foul ball. And I worked with him closely on some of these projects. And so I know what Bill Clinton was capable of, and I understood what Reagan was capable of. But that was a turning point. And that was the turning point that I experienced.

And since that time, *there has been no good President*, or Presidential candidate of any function in the United States. And our issue now, is to define what the requirements are of a valid President of the United States, which is not an offense against the foundation of the United States, from, shall we say, the great leader from New York (Alexander Hamilton).

And he *founded* this nation. He actually pulled it together, and got George Washington to pull it together, too. And that's how we got a United States. And we have been generally drifting up and down ever since, over the course of time.

But we can do it. *We can do it.* We have better resources than ever before. But only a few of us have them. Our job is to spread the knowledge that we have, and to spread it to more people, to create a unity of understanding among the people of the United States and elsewhere.

Q: Hi, Lyn, how's it going? We've been doing a lot of work in Brooklyn on this Italian question, back to the Italian standard we were discussing before. And quite generally we've been working to push the Verdi tuning more prevalently amongst a lot of the older Italian opera singers.

In fact, one of these Italian opera singers we met with earlier in the week, when briefed on our mobilization around the Verdi tuning, was very moved; she didn't just respond to the fact that the Verdi tuning was a better way of singing. But she got very moved because she knew that, "Ah, now you guys can do the *Va Pensiero*. And I can help teach you the *Va Pensiero*." So she was moved on that level, that now we can actually communicate the *idea* of the piece itself.

That same type of resonance around the music question, around the Verdi tuning is similar to what we're getting in the response around the concert we're doing

The Italian standard: Giuseppe Verdi conducting the Paris opera premier of Aida in 1880.

with the *Messiah* in Brooklyn, from the business owners and the people generally in the population. When we present it from the standpoint that we are going to use this, use the music question, as a counter to the homicides, the suicides, the police shootings, the mass killings, people are responding in a similarly moving way.

And I just wanted to get your feedback, on what the effect this is going to have on the population, generally?

The Italian Standard

LaRouche: Yes, I understand. The point is the Italian standard. Now I had been exposed in Italy, and was a participant in a celebration in honor of this work in Italy. And I was a participant in the centenary, in effect, of that period.

And the Italian standard, as defined by that standard, is probably the highest level of principled development of musical development, known to me. If anything matches that, it's not known to me. And so Verdi is the standard for *all good modern music*, as far as I know. The perfections are great.

Now the next thing, you would have other things—the Spanish thing is complicated, it's a mess; the French language is a mess to deal with in music: it's too much grunting and groaning involved there. And grunting and groaning is not good for the musical mind.

And so what Verdi represented *is* the standard which should be set,—*by Verdi's strict standards*, as such, is the standard for *all good music known to me*. If it's known to someone else, we'll have to talk about that. But Verdi's standard, as I experienced it at the celebration of his achievements—he was then dead, of course; and so, we went to his headquarters where he had lived; it was still his headquarters. And we had a great assembly among Italian musicians, and some Italian musicians who were also functioning from the United States and so forth. And we had this great event celebrating the work of Verdi. And that standard is still the best.

After the Italian, you have some German work, in

terms of poetry and things like that which are better. The French language is a grunting language, and it's a very bad language the way it's used. "Uhhnh, eehhnnn, hmm." Spanish similarly; Portuguese similarly. It does not produce good music. And there's some German music which is good, but Verdi is better. The Italian Verdi is much better. That's my knowledge.

EIRNS/Robert Wesser

The Schiller Institute's New York City Community chorus performing the Messiah in April of 2015.

Q: [follow-up] Just to follow up on that, what would you say the overall impact is going to be on the population, when we do more of this?

LaRouche: We're going to do it. And you know what we're going to do? We're going to take Manhattan—you may be acquainted with that locality. But that locality can be the proper place within the United States as such, within Manhattan, within the United States and bring in the Italian standard and the things that portend to the edge of the Italian Classical standard. That's the way to go.

And my conviction is that if we do that effectively,—and we do have some talent which can supply the training of some other people, who have some skills of their own talent now, and can acquire an improvement, copied on that talent,—we can actually change not only the quality of music in the United States and beyond, we can also create an improvement of the minds of the musicians now. Because by doing these things which are themselves beautiful and true, you make people stronger. You make them richer, in terms of what their lives mean to them and to the people around them.

So the idea of the retuning of music—shut down all this crap! Take the real standard required for competent musical composition. Associate yourself with the best people in terms of musicians, who could help to build the team of a new musical school, which is founded on the basis of, for example,—exemplary,—the Italian school of Verdi, and that itself will make things *much*

better. It'll make it much better in Italy, too....

Why the Manhattan Project

Q: Hi Lyn, it's A— here, in New York again. We have, as everyone knows, a weekend of concerts coming up, and the timing of this is no accident. The crucial importance of it is obvious to us. I've been, this past week, doing flyer distribution and talking to individuals about the *Messiah*, and I can't help but conclude, that as confused and as concerned as people are, the personal response I'm getting is that people welcome it and are open to attending. And I think we're going to have a very big turnout, at least from the Manhattan standpoint, and we still have another week of talking to people and making these distributions.

And one of the things that's kind of funny to me, not so much in the distributions, but just in conversations with people: we're having a heat wave up here, and several people have said to me—and I'm not kidding— "Yes, it's warm and that worries me." [laughs] And so, I said, "well, you know, we're singing Handel's *Messiah*"—I can't even get into the global warming thing with them!—I tell them what we're doing, and the response has been very, very good.

This is not just from boomers, these are younger people; I think the church that we're using is unknown to me, but very well known to people, and so, there is something different that is radiating from them. And you oftentimes wonder if it's you yourself that's kind of seeing this, but I don't think this was there before. And where we are with the silliness that people believe, and the insanity of the President, even though they won't talk about it, is something that's affecting them. so they're drawn to something like the *Messiah.*

My question to you is, now, once we complete this, I think we're going to be in a very strong position to catalyze people. And what is it that we should be looking to do, to make sure that that happens, and we can make Manhattan really grow?

LaRouche: Well, let's go back; in October of last year, I made a resolution to free the United States from the local states within it. And my conception was to look at what was focussed on Alexander Hamilton, and to take the Hamiltonian principle, which is a very useful one for all of these purposes, and to say, let us create, again, something which is consistent with the intention and the legacy of Classical musical composition. And what we did is, we found we were able to influence musicians, some of them who are first-rate musicians, performers, and others who are capable to be trained, to join the company of musical performers.

The idea is that. And this would go largely to the area of Manhattan and to certain areas around northern New Jersey, which are that; and to some limited degree, to Boston and so forth, there. So, my view has been that we should go full speed for this kind of program, on Classical music and related kinds of things. And with a great emphasis on the Classical composition work. That's what we've been doing.

Now, we've only got motion on this because we are bringing people together who are resolved to carry this out. The leading group of people around this group, are fully qualified for that talent. We have had experiments in education,—absolutely qualified. We've had successes. We simply need to get more perfection and more breadth and more depth in new areas of musical work; and people are coming to it. So this is particularly in the Manhattan region.

Now, my view has been that the idea of the United States as being the ruling institution, I said, that's crap! I know the Southern states of the United States, and most of them are crap. I know it; and many of them who are intelligent, also know it. but they go along with the local yokel stuff, and that local yokel commitment destroys their ability to fulfill any mission that they want to really get to. So therefore, my view is, we have Manhattan and the Manhattan area; and we have a spread into certain areas in New England and certain other locations. We can take what we have there as potential, serious potential, work on that, and spread that from that region, into the rest of the United States.

But the idea of the local yokel in the states is stupid. It doesn't work! It's wrong! You don't develop geniuses by training them to be fools. And that's the point. And so, what we've got in the Manhattan area, with a certain group around the northern parts of New Jersey, and you know what those regions are; and Brooklyn, of course, is always included in there; and we find that we have, in Manhattan and in the adjoining area there,—we have the potential of creating a choral organization, or a nest of choral organizations, which can bring a new spirit to the United States, through this vicinity. And we know you can't do the job efficiently, if you go at it in some other territories. You have to go in and colonize, these other states, and bring them to the reality of the purpose of their life.

Unite the Nations

Q: Hello, Lyn! I wanted to attempt a question regarding the impact of the Manhattan Project into the other parts of the nation. And from the standpoint, after a series of meetings with farmers and ag producers in Iowa and Illinois, last week, and the week before in Kansas and Missouri with cattlemen, what I've come to understand, as many people know, is that the state of the agriculture producers, is probably worse now than it was in the 1970s.

Cattle prices have dropped 51%; in 1973, the price of corn was $3.75 a bushel, and the price of good farmland was $700 [an acre]. Today, the average price of good farmland is $12,000-$15,000 an acre and the price of corn is—$3.75 a bushel.

So what you can see, is there's been a massive leveraging, and it's all coming from the Wall Street process, to the point where, now, the majority of the livestock produced in these areas, is under contracts with big packing plants which are all connected to the Wall Street banks. So in effect, what you've done is, you've moved the independent, owner-operator farm, into a process where the farmer's building buildings, providing the land, supporting the debt, and now he gets a fee, to work on his farm for a big packing plant of some kind; to raise crops for them, or livestock.

What that's done is that's brought into the understanding of almost everybody in agriculture, that this situation cannot continue. And what you see is, you see the most advanced technology, things that you would just think were only done by the rover on Mars, in terms of technology, is being used by the average high-tech farmer today, in putting in his crops with the GPS modern technology. So it's very productive and very efficient—except they're becoming slaves to a financial system.

Now, as a counter to that, the Manhattan Project has influenced some people, farmers in certain areas; and in one case, farmers who were facing a situation where their local church was going to be knocked down, and they fought that. Their ancestors came from Germany; they fought to keep it, and a couple farmers, after being connected with your type of thinking and the Manhattan Project and Classical music, set in motion to have Classical concerts in the church—which had never happened before, since it was erected.

And what happened is, the one farmer commented, he said, "I never saw so many grown men pull their hankies out" [pause] "and wipe tears out of their eyes."

I would like you to comment on that, in terms of the Manhattan Project's effect on the nation.

LaRouche: This is obvious, absolutely obvious. This is the course that we must take, there's no other course that's going to work. Agriculture, everything, the whole thing is one thing. All you have to do is say, "What did we lose? What was destroyed that we had, in terms of earlier generations and earlier decades of the population?" And when you look at that, and you look at what I saw while I was part of the Reagan Administration, in that period, there's been a general trend of degeneration, of the opportunities and resources, of the people of the United States.

We have to eliminate that discrepancy between the two values, and go beyond that in terms of progress, directly. We can do that and we *must* do that, and we must not accept anything *less* than that direction of achievement. It has to happen fast, it has to happen now, it's necessary to bring the nations in general, like the nations of Asia, like China, like India, like other nations in other parts of the world; in Africa, in other parts of that world; in South America, to bring South America and Central America and bring them back into a productive role of mankind.

We must do that on a global scale. We must bring

EIRNS/Robert Baker

Stacks of grain in the Kansas wheat belt—unable to move due to the collapse of the U.S. transportation grid.

those nations together for unification, of realizing, that is actually realizing, *physically realizing*, the reconstruction of the productive powers of labor, and of the human mind: That has to be done! That is a mission which we must never abandon. And we must keep going, once we've gotten to that point.

Q: Mr. LaRouche, good afternoon. R— from Brooklyn. In the past, you've talked about the Galactic coordinates; I've found in talking to people, various persons, college graduates, that global warming is not happening; that the education is so bad that I have to explain the Galactic coordinates. What do you think about this?

We Have a Mission to Perform

LaRouche: Well, of course, this is obvious. The point is, since the beginning of, well, shall we say, the Reagan Administration, the first part of the Reagan Administration, before the Bush family really got moved in there, there's been a consistent degeneration. See, the last time we had an achievement was when I won a victory, in Manhattan, at the beginning, in 1971, and we won then on that case, and we've been losing ever since. And when I came into the Presidency, under the Presidency of Ronald Reagan, it was a part of a middle area, when we still had the potential, at that point, of getting progress again.

But when Reagan was actually almost killed by an asscoiate of the Bush family, the trend has been *downward* ever since. And the rate of downwardness has tended to be predominantly an increasing rate of stupidity, the destruction of ideas.

So therefore, once we take that into account, we have a mission to perform. It's a mission which mankind demands for the sake of mankind as such. We cannot accept anything less. And it is achievable! It is an achievable event!

Q: [follow-up] I take it that if the Manhattan project is successful, we will have an effect on the educational system?

LaRouche: Absolutely. That's the only answer. That's the only possibility.

Q: Mr. LaRouche, it's W— from the Bronx. I just wanted to know, what do you think about Trump and a lot of his influence here in New York City?

LaRouche: I think a Trump is an insult against elephants. He's a kind of animal we don't want, a Trump. And a Trump is also a piece of folly, even in the gambling business.

Now, I hope that makes your day sweeter.

Q: [follow-up] Yes, thank you. Thank you. A lot of my friends seem to like him, and I don't understand them.

Speed: Wow—well, we all have friends like that. The ones we need to "unfriend!" [laughter]

Q: Or uplift!

LaRouche: How are you, young man?

Speed: Well, I have a story for you. There is a recent movie made, and there is an earlier documentary, about the August 1974 walk between the two towers of the World Trade Center. There was a Frenchman, 24 years old, who one night, with a team, put a wire up between the two Towers; and he walked for 45 minutes between the two Towers. *Except*, when the police went to apprehend him—and there is documentary footage of the actual policeman speaking in 1974,—he said, "well, he wasn't really walking. The only thing that you can say is that he was dancing."

Now, when this was said at the time, when I saw it, I just thought, well, there was somehow an athletic

creative commons/Galaxy fm

Philippe Petit walks across a tightrope suspended between the World Trade Center's Twin Towers in August 1974.

achievement. No! Because the wire-walker explained, in a brief discussion, he said, "No, well, there's a technical name for this, it's called a catenary, but let me just tell you what I did." And so he goes on and never says more.

But he had learned the technique—he was not a member of a circus. He had studied various circuses, and he also was a bit of an artist himself; he did a lot of drawings of a lot of different constructions. But I only bring this up because of what you were saying earlier about the rope dance, and the fact that there are people who *knew* this, and that this is something that *is* known and is a physical knowledge that people have. I thought I would just tell you that.

We're looking for the gentleman who did it; he happens to live in New York City these days, to see what he might have to say about all this.

So I just wanted to tell you that story.

I guess, if there are no other questions, we have a choral rehearsal and other things we have to do this evening. So Lyn, I'd like you to give us some final remarks and we'll get to work.

LaRouche: OK, that's a good idea! Well, I think I have done my speaking on this question today. And I think it's something which, by its nature, is something which demands a continuity of realization. And so, I hope what we've done so far in terms of this particular session, will be something which will lead to a profitable benefit for the people who were involved in this work.

Speed: OK! Well, thank you. So on behalf of everybody here: Thank you very much, Lyn. Let's let Lyn know we appreciate what he just did for us. [applause]

The Force of Unity Is The Secret of Humanity

Dec. 14—Directly after his Dec. 12 dialog with Manhattan activists reported above, Lyndon LaRouche began a 50-minute colloquy with a group in Alameda County in northern California, chaired by LaRouche PAC Policy Committee member Michael Steger. LaRouche's talk was followed by presentations by former U.S. Senator from Alaska Mike Gravel, agriculturalist Eric Wilson, and LaRouche PAC Science Team leader Benjamin Deniston. Only LaRouche's part of the meeting is reported here.

Michael Steger: So, Lyn, this is Michael. We've got an audience here for you gathered in Alameda, California, and we're very excited to hear what you have to say, so, without further introduction, I think you should just go ahead and start the proceedings.

Lyndon LaRouche: Okay. Let's do it. I'm ready whenever the closure is established. Why don't you speak to me first, and then announce....

Steger: Would you like to start with questions, or would you like to give a short introduction?

LaRouche: Let's start questions and then we'll go back into the discussion.... get the questions lined in there so I get a feeling of what exactly you want. Sometimes it's implicit to what should be wanted, and therefore if you start with an opening discussion, then you get into the meat of the substance.

Q: Mr. LaRouche, my name is K— from Sunnyvale, CA, and the question I have is, I know that there is a large move to impeach President Obama, and I just received a certified letter from, I believe, it's the United States Justice Foundation, and they're asking me to send money, of course, and also a petition. This is a group of what you'd call Republican, if you will, or right-wing folks who feel that President Obama should be impeached. My question to you is, how can we all join forces together to get this to happen?

Immediate Action to Save the Nation

LaRouche: First of all, we have two major parties, Democratic and Republican. Now some of the Republicans are no damn good, and some of the Democrats are no damn good, but, as I've laid it out earlier this week, the point is we have to bring together, urgently, the sane people—not Trump—but the sane people among the Republicans and Democrats who actually are sincerely dedicated, to grope quickly through what they have to do to bring about an immediate end to the Obama Administration.

The extinction of the Obama Administration is the absolute requirement, prerequisite, for saving the United States. And the history of the United States is to take large bodies, political bodies, and people, and bring them together to get into a discussion. The discussion involves differ-

creative commons/Gage Skidmore

The fact that we can all recognize that Trump is no damn good, is a great motive for bringing sane Republicans and Democrats together. Here, Trump at CPAC in 2013.

16   Shut Wall Street This Week

EIR   December 18, 2015

ences, it involves positives, it involves changes in behavior all the way through. We want to take, no matter what the meat is of the Republicans, if they're honest and sincere about being Republicans, and being part of the Democratic-Republican organization, we want those people, because it is only when we begin to get that discussion, that we will find that we have the ability to get the mechanics of bringing people into actual cooperation.

Because they don't know what they want. They think they know what they want, but they don't know, because they have not tested the question, they have not tested the matter, and they have to do an exploratory process with the understanding that they are going to try to work on it. The *sane* Republicans and the *sane* Democrats will go to work and say "We've got to save this nation right now." We're not going to give it to Obama, we're not going to give it to a foreign party, we will negotiate with foreign organizations which are relevant, but we are not,—we have got to make a probe, a seriously dedicated probe to bring together the right Republicans and the right Democrats, without much discretion. We just want sincerity.

We know that Trump is no damn good. So the reason that we all can recognize that Trump is no damn good, is the great motive for bringing the *sane* Democrats and the *sane* Republicans back together, to begin, urgently, a program to define how we are going to get out of this mess. And the mess right now is that we're on the edge of general thermonuclear warfare. We're on the edge of that right now. So if we sit there as Democrats and Republicans as separate groups, it's not going to work, because you're not going to be able to deliver the job on time.

So, therefore, we have to bring the Democrats and the Republicans who are sane, bring them quickly into negotiation, with the intent to create a solid basis for the United States policy. We have to go through that experience. We're going to have to go with quick action and solid action, and with a process of patient discovery of things we have to quickly discover and settle. And once we get into this discussion, which I suppose we can have here now from my standpoint,—from what my thoughts are, what the contribution has to be,—we want to make this thing national and we want to make it in effect.

But we realize we need the urgent reform of both the Democratic and Republican Parties, and then we can bring broader areas among the citizens into play. Once

we can make some sense of bringing the two, the Republican and Democratic Parties together, sane ones, then we can go to a further step quickly, and begin to get some broad terms. And there are senior people in both parties who can come quickly to bringing forth proposals for immediate action to save this nation from the threat of general thermonuclear war.

Q: Mr. LaRouche, this is B— from Fair Oaks, Sacramento County, and I was interested in the 25th Amendment and a rapid removal of President Obama, as President Nixon was removed, and I've seen it can happen in one day, coming from the top people from the Democratic Party in this case, as it was done in the case of President Nixon. How can this come about and the right people not make the excuses and denials as I come across?

Where we live, in our district, the 7th Congressional District, Congressman Dr. Ami Bera answers like a lawyer, just picks stuff apart and denies there ever was treason or any reason for Obama to be impeached or removed by the 25th Amendment,—that's just a field caseworker for this guy. I've gone 23 times to that office, and they're just liars, and deniers; it's useless. So I'd like to know, how could it happen?

A Common Interest Faced with the Enemy
LaRouche: You can solve the problem by going on with the discussion of what should be. Because, right now, anybody who is sane in the Democratic and Republican Parties, given this proposal, will, if they are sane, accept it immediately.

Why? Because they don't know what they are going to do, but what they do know is that if we can't bring a Republican faction and Democratic faction into a common interest approach, we are not going to accomplish anything under these circumstances. So therefore, you are starting with a Republican and Democratic Party who have been normally at odds on principle. We know that that is no good. We just assume that members of the Congress are honest representatives of what we believe the interests of the United States are. They're going to come to an agreement, an urgent agreement, an immediate urgent agreement to create the first step to create a formal meeting, an open continued meeting, between the relevant Republicans and the relevant Democrats.

Because if we are going to get into a fuss of trying to deal with our problems, which come from foreign sources, we have to have a unity among the leading forces of our government in the United States. And we have to get something which resembles a fair approximation of the people we want to initiate with, as the initiatives which are going to create this new arrangement in the Congress, a unity action by the Democrats and Republicans. Then we can come quickly to certain steps,—which will not be the completed steps, but initial steps which will bring the spirit and heart of the Democratic and Republican Party sections to a certain unity for action.

White House/Pete Souza

Two evil British agents, Saudi King Salman and U.S. President Obama, meeting in Riyadh, Saudi Arabia on Jan. 27, 2015.

Now, we had the case, where you had a Presidential candidate, Alexander Hamilton, and Hamilton went through the process, in Pennsylvania, of creating, bringing together people in proper order, and as a result of that, we had the founding of the United States Constitution. We're looking at something which is comparable to that in a certain manner of speaking, something that you can think about, what happened when he introduced the idea of creating the Government.

You're in that kind of situation. We're trying to re-establish the principle of the Constitution, but we haven't got a Constitution yet, not really. We're going to have to get one, we're going to have to get one quickly, because we've got to get Obama out of this business quickly. If you can bring the Democratic and Republican leaderships together, even on this open option, you can win, you can get Obama out of office. Obama is a hateful creature inherently. And it's only as long as the Democrats and Republicans can be at loggerheads with each other on these things that Obama can continue to exist.

The bringing together of the relevant leaders of the Democratic and Republican Parties will eliminate Obama. If we do that, you will have a chance of surviving. If you don't do that, you probably—the United States—will not survive. And that's what we're playing at. We're not talking about negotiating this or that and so forth. Bunk! No! I know about politicians, and politi-

cians have screwball ideas from my standpoint, because they don't come to an actual principle. They come to a negotiating argument. This is no time for negotiations, as such, except the idea of looking for a common interest in face of the enemy. And the enemy is, in particular, the British Empire, and Obama. And Obama is nothing but an agent of the British Empire.

And we've got to save the United States. If we save the United States in this fashion, we can save the world. If we don't.... Because Russia will play the game, others will play the game, China will play the game, India will play the game, others, and we can bring about a new condition on the basis of what the original intention was on the formation of the United States under the leadership and prompting of Alexander Hamilton.

From that standpoint, we have an option. The world is, in large degree, ready for that option. We've got some evil forces running loose. We've got to shut them down. The way you do it, is you create a unity of the viable people as a force who understand they must solve the problems which are involved with this now. Do it promptly! Not a long-winded debate, but we've got to meet quickly and say, "What is our purpose?" and the one thing you have to say is, "it ain't Obama!"

Q: Mr. LaRouche, it's an honor to speak with you. When I see you, I'm reminded of Shakespeare's sonnet, in which he says, "To me, fair friends, you never can be old." And that's true of you and of Helga, and just to be in this company, and it's Mindy Pechenuk's birthday today, it's such a great day! And I love you so much, and I'm especially heartened to hear of all the choirs and choruses that are now being formed in Manhattan.

I would like to hear how the classical culture, and development of the literature and art and music, could you speak on the role of that in bringing,—because it is a common denominator of Republicans and Democrats, they love Classical music—how can Classical culture support this goal of getting the two parties together to have a common cause in defeating Obama and bringing in a renaissance? Thank you.

Not a Deal but a Passion

LaRouche: Well the key element of this process, what you referred to on this account, is music, Classical music. Because if you can take the spirit of Classical music as we are doing it in Manhattan,—what we're doing, we are bringing together, according to, largely, principally, the Italian source, the original Italian source, and by doing that, and we still know some of the people who are alive in the time that I knew when the Italian musical program existed and I participated in that area. And we had some good times with it.

But once you get that idea, that you're coming together on the basis of certain things that you really agree with, and are willing to agree with because you feel you're safe with—Because the problem is, can you trust people? Can you trust a Democrat, can you trust a Republican? Offhand, no. As a matter of fact, a Democrat can't consort with a Democrat or a Republican with a Republican, or almost anything like that.

You have to come to a point of affinity which is not merely an opinion as such, but to a definition of urgency; and we are in an extremely urgent situation, probably the most urgent situation to happen to all mankind so far. We're on the edge of thermonuclear war, global thermonuclear war. Obama is the agent of the British and other interests for thermonuclear war. We're on the edge of it, now!

Therefore, at this time, if we sit there with Democrats and Republicans separating, as they are,—not just getting angry with each other, but the way they are,— they cannot come to the kind of decision which has the authority, common authority, to move quickly, to necessary emergency actions to occur, on the presumption we are going to continue on that process to a more re-fined quality of development. We need that spirit, we need the confidence of the citizens of the United States to believe that the leadership of the Congress, of the best part of the leadership of the Congress, is prepared to act on that basis. And we have to ask, "Will you, the Presidency, will you come to that emergency agreement right now? Because if you won't, we're finished. If you do, we can probably win."

I mean, this is not something like a deal, a trade-off deal. That's not it; it's something more. We're going to a period now, where the very potential of the explosions happening throughout the planet, as now,—and if you don't change this climate, political climate, globally, you're not going to save it at all.

The time has come to get emergency leadership which becomes not only a kernel of the international leadership of the nations, and that beginning will turn, what? Away from Obama, who is an agency of the British monarchy, the British system. That's all he is. He's also Satanic, but that's another aspect of him. And therefore, we have to create it in the United States, because we have to do it; if we don't bring the Republicans and Democrats together in a certain way, in this way, of saying, "Drop this nonsense you've been playing. We've got a common interest which we must protect and support."

You've got to get a sense of unity, a sense of passion for survival of our nation and this meaning, and the other nations which are also jeopardized, with China, with Japan. We've seen success in Japan, again. We see it in other parts. We see it in India, we see it in other locations. If we can do that in the United States now, by consolidating, as I have just indicated here, the unity of the Congress, as Alexander Hamilton did, to create the unity of the Congress, despite some evil members of the Congress itself. And we need that.

This is not a deal. This is a passion which is demanded by all leading minds. We must stop this nonsense! We can have a fresh shot at the United States being reconstructed. We want to stick to the original Hamiltonian view of the formation of the United States. We want to reach out to other nations and other parts of the world. We want to bring these nations together, and bring the United States together, to bring the United States together in cooperation with other nations, to create a unity of nations. Because we are not in the business of trade-offs.

The human species is unique. The human species is not a collection of animals. There's a big difference, despite a lot of opinions to the contrary. And therefore, what we have to do is we have to bring together the leading features of the United States' power, to bring together our citizens to a sense of unity, radiated around that. We have to do that on the basis of reaching out to China, to India, to other locations. We have to bring a kind of unity of the human spirit, because the human spirit right now is in pretty bad condition.

But if we start, as the United States started, under Hamilton's leadership, we can save this nation, and by saving this nation, and working with it, we can save humanity from what Obama is trying to bring upon it.

Willing to Sacrifice Your Foolishness?

Q: Hello, Lyn; this is Pat Ruckert. Haven't seen you for a while, but in the 45 years I've been associated with you, one of your constant reminders—to put it in mild terms—is to remind us again and again and again of the principles and the ideas that you're trying to get across and accomplish. And what you've said so far I think is a good example of that; the unity of the sane Republicans and the sane Democrats towards saving the nation.

And I think yesterday or the day before, you actually put some real meat on that by saying that we have to repeat what happened in 1933, when Republicans and Democrats united around the leader, Franklin Roosevelt, and implemented the Glass-Steagall Act, which busted Wall Street. And I'd like you to actually just talk a little bit about that, because it really gives a sense of the difference between a Wall Street economy and a production economy.

LaRouche: A Wall Street economy, which is now operating in the United States as the ruling model, will destroy the entire United States and crush it, and lead to its extinction. Therefore, the main thing is, we have to shut down Wall Street with no compensation; because the compensation involves thievery, pure outright thievery. Cancel it! Take Glass-Steagall and use the Franklin Roosevelt Glass-Steagall approach; put that into effect, and you don't pay off anybody in terms of Wall Street.

That's our problem; Wall Street is what makes us prisoners. And the British give the orders, and Wall

NSHS

Bipartisan collaboration for the nation: Republican Nebraska Sen. George Norris, a key promoter of the TVA, campaigns for FDR's re-election campaign in 1936.

Street carries them out. What we have to do is, we have to bring back the idea of the unity of purpose of the United States. The unity of purpose—what's that? Look at the condition of our citizens; look at them! Aren't they being destroyed? Aren't the farmers being destroyed? Aren't people being murdered by drugs which are induced upon them, by the conditions of life under which they work? Are we not aware of the destruction of the forces of production which the United States used to represent, which have now been made into jellyfish? Stinking jellyfish at that.

We have to create this unity of what the United States represented as Alexander Hamilton exemplified. And once you understand that, that you've got a bunch of people apart from certain Senators, certain members of the Congress, who are skunks; as a matter of fact, we had four skunks right after the first two Presidents. But we get rid of the skunks. But we know what the intention was, as Alexander Hamilton made it very clear; the four conditions of productivity. His four conditions of productivity; that's a good beginning for any agreement. You get the Congress pulled together, the Senate, the House of Representatives; that's your start automatically, one of your great starts.

You want agriculture? We need agriculture; but who's taking it away from us? It's Wall Street; and what Wall Street represents—and Obama. So, if we can unify things around these kinds of elementary issues—I mean not elementary by being stupid, but elementary because you can't succeed without them. Certain changes have to occur. You can say, "Wait for other things; wait for other things."; but there are certain things that must be brought together now! Otherwise, you don't win, you lose.

Every crisis in mankind that I've known of, has always come to the point where, "What are you willing to give up to gain what you must get?" What foolishness can man separate himself from, for the sake of gaining the most precious things for all humanity? Alexander Hamilton brought this on creating what became the United States.

Q: Good afternoon, sir. My name is D—; I'm from San Jose, California. My question right now is how do you propose—well, first, pulling together honest Democrat and Republican representatives, Congressmen; it depends on assuming that there are some. I'm not sure that's really valid; but if there are, they're all so used to, and so motivated by re-election that they're slaves to Wall Street and big corporations on both sides. So, they need the money to finance their re-election campaigns.

So, all I'm saying is, the last time I know of when both sides of the country actually pulled together to defeat a common enemy was what I heard about happened in World War II. And I'm just saying, is there any way we can feed on that patriotism that there used to be; or there was some of that when John Kennedy was alive? Can we use that to avoid World War III? That's my question.

Get Obama Out!

LaRouche: That's my point. And that's why I say, if you bring together a core of the Democrats and Republicans on the basis that I've laid out in the past days, you will solve the problem. Now the question is, what kind of solution are you getting? What you're getting is the fact that the necessity of the Glass-Steagall policy is obvious; without Glass-Steagall, there is no solution. Because right now, the condition of the planet in terms of things like no Glass-Steagall in the United States and similar kinds of things in Europe and so forth; under those conditions, you haven't got a chance. We haven't got a chance.

So therefore, we have to go with the core question: How are we going to go back to the promise that was made by Alexander Hamilton, and simply get the job done? And if you look at Hamilton's writings, all you have to do is take the published writings of Alexander Hamilton, especially the four principles that he raised

on the economic question, and that is the solution. Now, you have to perfect the solution; you have to understand what the solution meant. You've got to understand what it means in practice.

We are now killing our citizens; this is already in process. The farmers are being killed, or being destroyed in terms of their claims. We've got to change that! You need to find a keystone which will actually present the mechanism which will bring it together. And my estimate is, if you could bring some of the Republicans and some of the Democrats, a very large number, to understand exactly what the issue is,—we can win. Because we will throw Obama out, automatically.

The first thing that the Congress will do under those conditions, is throw Obama out of office immediately. The mood is already on the edge; because Obama is producing more and more evil. You've got to shut it down; and the way to do that is if the Republican and Democratic Parties are not played against each other; then, Obama is dumped. And if you don't dump Obama, you're going to have Obama-ism; and under Obama-ism, you don't have a chance. Get him out of the street! He's killing people every Tuesday; Obama is killing citizens of the United States every Tuesday. And you're sitting back and not doing anything about it? You're accepting that kind of goings-on? What do you expect?

I'm telling you, if you get the Republican and Democratic Parties hating some evil people, including that Republican who's being dumped, and Hillary, who should be dumped.... Get those elements out; and get a negotiation between the relevant Republicans and Democrats. And out of the sense of desperation, they will say, "I don't know about that; I guess we've got to do it." And that's what you want.

Q: Hello, Lyn. This is N— from Oakland. I've been listening to your encouragement, your demands, and I'm trying to not put your demands off on some other neighbor of mine; but to require your request, demand that I do something important. We have among us here in Alameda, a man who's done that in the past—Senator Mike Gravel; he'll be speaking with us soon.

I, through my life shortly past, meaning last July, ran across an article that's come back to me frequently since then. It was an article introducing me to a man who was responsible for the exposure of Cointelpro, as I'm certain you're familiar with, having been a victim of those operations. His name is John Raines, who came out recently and exposed that he was one of eight among those who broke into the Media [Pennsylvania] FBI of-

White House/Pete Souza

Obama at the desk where he decides on his "kill list" every Tuesday. This was taken on Thanksgiving Day, 2015.

fices. He's quite active; he's an octogenarian, like most actual living patriots. Meaning to say, if you're an octogenarian, you have a more reasonable chance of being a patriot. I'm speaking to you today to, one, identify John Raines and his current work.

I'm speaking in part to push myself to confront him to join us; and to do something which not too many years ago, even while participating in your organization, I would not have thought that I would be willing to do: To confront that level of courage displayed by others in the past. I've been quite rowdy with my U.S. Representative Barbara Lee, but I have yet to get her to move and act consistent with what I believe her heartfelt intent is. So, in a public venue, I'm kicking myself in the ass, and saying, "Get going, Ned. You've got work to do." And I thank you for that, and your leadership and your encouragement, and your direction of how to be effective in my function. Thank you.

LaRouche: Thank you as well.

The Idea is the Only Real Solution

Q: Mr. LaRouche, this is —. I've been in recent years echoing your sentiments to just about everybody I encounter; at Mucky's [ph] standing in line, and among good friends I've known for years. And I've developed one follower for you and what we're all about. Ninety-nine percent of my friends are "burn him off;" they don't want to listen to me go on and on. They just don't get it. And try as I might—which is all the time—I'm sad-

dened by getting no place most of the time.

But anyway, today I hear what you have to share with us about accessing a nucleus of both major parties, and having grasped the gravity and reality of the situation and start doing something about it. The trick is, I'm a voice in the wilderness that has been ignored like howling at the moon a lot; but we have with us Mike Gravel, a Senator in Alaska some while ago. And he did some miraculous brave things that counted and had effect. We need people of that caliber to approach what can become the nucleus of this united team, I think.

For me to continue to howl at the moon at the level of involvement which is practically nil, on the part of people that don't even vote, or don't know anything about what's going on—don't care—again, howling at the moon. But if we can identify and access people—I had my picture taken several years ago at an event with former Secretary of Defense Perry. I could probably show him that picture, and he'd say, "Yeah, I kind of remember that." But he doesn't know me; I know him, he's famous. "Yeah, I remember that picture being taken, but who are you?"

But we need people who are instrumental; I think he's still very active behind the scenes. So, maybe those movers and shakers who are not currently in office, because the people now who are striving to get elected are busy striving to get elected. They're preoccupied with trying to become the President. There are others, either on their team, or I don't know. We need to get,—we, being you and your followers,—need to get to people who are influential to pull this nucleus together. I see it, I get it; but I'm just one guy....

LaRouche: The point is that the idea is the only real solution; and the idea has to be the right idea. Because otherwise people find themselves inept; incapable of even the most precious dreams that they have. Because they say, "Yes, that's sweet. It's a sweet song, but who can sing it?" And that's the point.

You have to concentrate, as I have done, because of my international activities and so forth at least in former times, and that's how you do it. You take some basic ideas, the most fundamental ideas which mankind has said, "Well, no; that will never work. That will never work; that will never work." And I've had a success in life on the basis that I've known what does work; as opposed to things that some people thought would never work.

Right now, we have a great crisis in the United States and throughout the planet. We have to bring a new state of affairs among nations and among people; because we cannot continue this way. And the real facts are, that we cannot live this way; that's the force which impels people to seek the actual secret, which never was a secret except when people hid it from themselves.

Unity is the Secret of Humanity

Q: Mr. LaRouche, I have a quick follow-up question. A couple of years ago, I was at the Republican state convention in Sacramento. I attended a Tea Party caucus, and Congressman Tom McClintock was the speaker. And at the end of his talk, I arose and challenged him: where was that one person in our Congress who had the guts to impeach President Obama?

Now ironically, I just found out a couple of days ago, that House Resolution 198 was introduced in April by Congressman Yoho from Florida; and lo and behold, a co-sponsor of that bill, one of two, is Congressman McClintock.

So, my question is, it seems to me that this bill has no co-sponsors from the Democratic side; all Republicans. And there are people who are raving in the Tea Party group, just rambling to say they got to get rid of this guy; it just seems so inconceivable why we can't join, as I said earlier in my question, why can't we join together just as you are suggesting? And the real question I have is, who do you feel are those key people that we need to contact right now?

LaRouche: The short answer is, sometimes you should know that, but you didn't see it. In other words, the point is now that the whole system is with absolute certainty on the rail of destruction. This lies not only in the Democratic and Republican Parties, it lies with the nation as a whole; and it lies in a certain way, with the planet as a whole—from the top down. And therefore, when you realize that you don't have to bargain with somebody, when you know you have won the case.

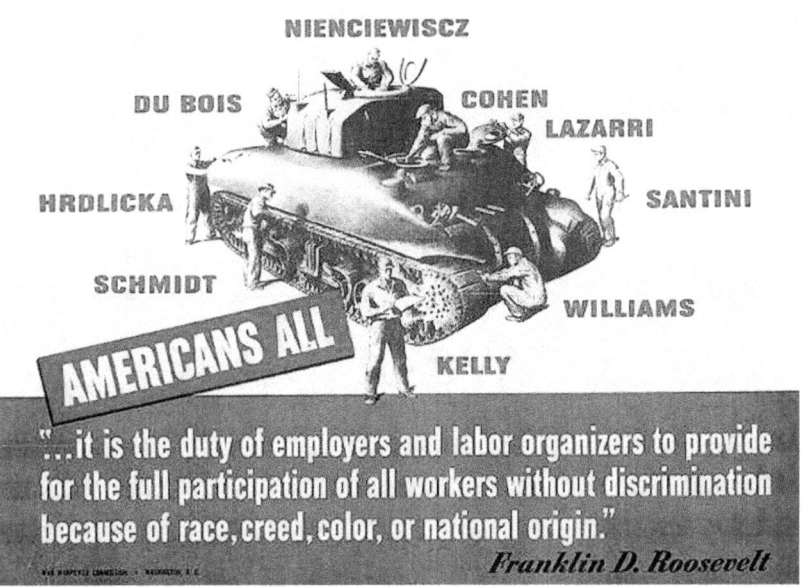

Library of Congress

National Unity: A government poster from 1942, during the mobilization for World War II.

Now, if you didn't know the case and couldn't win it, that unity of purpose does not work.

But if you proceed from the standpoint of knowing what the facts are, to understand people and to understand nations, as I have worked with it.... When you know those ideas, you've been through nations after nations, which I've worked with. And I find "Yes, yes, yes."

I've also seen my dearest friends assassinated in various parts of the planet; and those assassinations tell me exactly what the problem is. Why were they killed? Like Indira Gandhi; why was she murdered by the British? Why? Because she was a genius; and genius is what these guys specify as a target for killing. Indira Gandhi; that's not the only case. There are many cases of leading figures who were assassinated; again and again. De Gaulle was not assassinated; but he was virtually assassinated before he died. Because the fascist party, which is called the Socialist Party in France, is the force of evil. Obama is the force of evil.

And therefore, the question is, if you've got an option, you better do something about it quickly; because the forces of Satan will gather quickly, exterminate you, and then go back to business as they were doing it before. Unity; the force of unity, is the secret of humanity.

Steger: Lyn, you've been more than generous with your time today, so we very much appreciate it. And we wish you good will, and we'll talk to you again soon.

LaRouche: Thank you.

U.S. AND RUSSIA MUST WORK TOGETHER

Only a New Paradigm Can Prevent Fascism!

by Helga Zepp-LaRouche
Chair of the German political party Civil Rights Movement Solidarity

Dec. 12—With the world more and more out of joint, it is becoming increasingly obvious that not only is sticking with the old paradigm of Anglo-American-dominated globalization increasing the acute risk of world war with every passing day, but that fascist 'solutions' are being prepared, or already being implemented, on both sides of the Atlantic.

But neither the extinction of mankind in a thermonuclear Armageddon, nor the sacrifice of human life for the benefit of the financial oligarchy are inevitable. Preventing this, however, will require overcoming partisanship and geopolitics, and replacing them with nonpartisan cooperation at all levels, for the common aims of mankind.

The European agency for controlling the EU's borders, commonly known as Frontex, interrogates a would-be immigrant.

It is no surprise that the European Union (EU), which, since its founding by the Maastricht Treaty, has turned into a monster, and is now, in the face of the refugee crisis and the impending financial crash, not only exposed as a failed model, but is implementing an openly fascist policy. The most recent thrust in this direction is the Brussels announcement of a plan to replace the already abominable EU border control organization Frontex with a new organization controlled by Brussels, which will use its own border guards to deport refugees.

Reports are that the organization would even be able to operate in states that are not members of the EU, and that the EU could disregard objections by member states. Thus the refugee issue would lead to the largest transfer of sovereignty to Brussels since the introduction of the euro.

The very idea that Europe could be shielded by new 'Limes' fortifications by force of arms, while Southwest Asia and Africa are sinking into war, chaos, and poverty, is just as moronic as it is inhumane.

Eating Its Own

But anyone who thinks the EU monster is using this policy to protect the people living within the Limes walls is very much mistaken.

For example, the EU Commission is now threatening Italy with legal action, because the Italian government only partially applied to four bankrupt banks the "bail-in law" already adopted by all EU members—the so-called Cyprus-model—in combination with a "bailout." Despite this compromise, many of these banks' customers lost all their deposits. In this context, a 68-year-old retiree from Civitavecchia, who lost his life savings in Banca Etruria, committed suicide. The State Prosecutor is now investigating whether there was incitement to suicide.

As is now known, the Italian central bank had opposed the European Central Bank's demands for a full bail-in by the bank's depositors, and instead used money from the Italian Deposits Guarantee Fund for a bailout. There is fierce opposition in Germany to extending this bailout mechanism to the European level (European Deposits Guarantee Fund), because of course, it is primarily German depositors and taxpayers who would have to pay. The Italian bail-in gives a foretaste of the expropriation of citizens' savings which the EU has up its sleeve for the new, imminent financial crash.

The bottom line: The EU is neither a Union nor does it have a "European Idea" within it; it has neither a concept for solving the refugee crisis nor for defending the common good of the citizens of the EU. The only interests it protects are those of the financial oligarchy and the EU's bloated bureaucracy. The faster this monster is dismantled, and the sovereign nation-states of Europe put a stop to the casino economy,—through reintroducing a Glass-Steagall-style banking separation law, reviving the real economy with a new credit system and working with Russia and China to solve existential problems,—the better it will be.

Two Factions in the United States

On the other side of the Atlantic, more and more influential figures are convinced that neither the United States nor the rest of the world will survive if Obama remains Commander-in-Chief for his remaining 13 months in office. It is an open secret in informed circles that Obama personally gave his backing—sometimes not even just implicitly—for the ongoing provocations against Russia and China: from Turkey's shootdown of the Russian bomber over Syria, to the

youtube/RT

Former DIA chief Michael Flynn speaking to press in Moscow, where he attended a Russia Today conference on Dec. 10, 2015.

deployment of U.S. Special Forces and Turkish troops in Iraq, to the bombing of Syrian Army soldiers by the U.S. Air Force.

In the latest live fire intercept test of Aegis Ashore, the U.S. Navy and the Missile Defense Agency successfully destroyed a ballistic missile target at the Pacific Missile Range Facility in Hawaii. The test also demonstrated the Aegis Ashore system's capability to interact with other radar systems, which greatly extends the integrated shield of defense that the Aegis system provides both at sea and on land.

This system, like the entire U.S. missile defense system, the Prompt Global Strike doctrine, and the Air-Sea Battle doctrine, is geared toward being able to deliver a first strike against the nuclear second strike capabilities of both Russia and China. The Russian military has stated repeatedly in the clearest terms, that they cannot and will not allow these systems to be built up to the extent that Russia becomes defenseless. And that point is very close.

Concern that the point of no return in the confrontation with Russia may soon be reached, is the context for recent articles calling for activation of the 25th Amendment to the U.S. Constitution,—namely, the clause that is invoked if the President is no longer able to perform the duties of his office for physical or mental reasons. (See, for example, the article by Charles Hurt, "The Nuclear Option: Is It Time to Invoke the 25th Amendment?"

No less great is the dread within the Republican

Party leadership at the seemingly unstoppable campaign success of Donald Trump, whose fascist-leaning demagogy has already dashed the prospects of Wall Street favorite Jeb Bush. The Republican so-called powerbrokers fear a sweeping election defeat if Trump wins the nomination.

In America there are currently two clearly distinct groups. On the one side there are the utopian hawks, who indulge the illusion that a combination of provocation and technological victory in the arms race will enable them to force Russia and China to their knees—risking the thermonuclear annihilation of the human species. On the other side are those who insist that the world's existential problems can only be solved if the United States, Russia, and China work together. The latter position is supported by the former head of the U.S. Defense Intelligence Agency, Gen. Michael Flynn (ret.), as well as all rational people in Europe.

A Global Threat

The Islamic State terrorist organization operates worldwide; it threatens every country on Earth, but especially Europe, Russia, China, and the United States, from which it is continually recruiting jihadists. This will continue as long as it has a territorial base of operations, which is in reality made possible by Western "allies" Turkey and Saudi Arabia.

Sharon Premoli, one of the few survivors of the attack of Sept. 11, 2001, issued a scathing attack on the Obama Administration in the *Huffington Post* on Dec. 8, saying that the Administration still calls Saudi Arabia an ally, even though it is the real power that finances the propaganda apparatus that disseminates Wahhabi-Salafist ideology through all the radical mosques worldwide. Those who allow themselves to be bought by Saudi money could only be described as the Nazi collaborators of the Twenty-first Century.

In Germany, the insanity of delivering heavy weapons to states such as Saudi Arabia and Turkey, which support ISIS, must stop. It is both cynical and criminal to offer Turkey billions of dollars to hold back the refugees who are the victims of this policy.

Lyndon LaRouche has called for a non-partisan coalition to come together to take all necessary measures to save the United States. These include strategic cooperation with Russia and China, the introduction of the Glass-Steagall Act, and the return of the United States to its identity as a Republic.

In Europe as well, and especially in Germany, overcoming hidebound party politics and forming a nonpartisan coalition for Reason is absolutely essential. The way out of the refugee crisis and the threat of a new financial meltdown lies in cooperation with the BRICS countries: building the New Silk Road, a global program of economic cooperation which would develop Southwest Asia and Africa economically so that people would no longer need to flee from war, famine, and chaos. Only if we quickly place this new paradigm on the agenda, and put the common aims of mankind ahead of narrow or presumed national interests, does mankind have a chance to survive.

The admonition expressed by the United States' first president, George Washington, in his 1796 farewell speech, also applies to us today: Those who value party politics more than they do their loyalty to the principles of the Republic, embody the serious danger of "a frightful despotism." It is the interest and duty of wise people to discourage and curb this partisan thinking.

Are there enough people in the United States, in Germany, France, and Italy, with the courage and foresight to conduct a public discourse about these issues, and turn things around in time?

This article was translated from German.

Unsurvivable

A dark, gruesome, but wholly true depiction of the threat of thermonuclear war, its consequences, and Obama's deployment of a major portion of the U.S. thermonuclear capabilities in multiple theaters threatening both Russia and China.

http://larouchepac.com/unsurvivable

President Obama Boosted Muslim Brotherhood

by Jeffrey Steinberg

Dec 15—President Barack Obama has boosted the Muslim Brotherhood as a "moderate" force within "political Islam" from the beginning of his first term in office.

That policy grew, and continued, until late 2012, when the Mohammed Morsi/Muslim Brotherhood government in Egypt launched a brutal crackdown on political dissenters and refused to create a broader ruling coalition.

Even after tens of millions of Egyptians turned out on the streets of Cairo and other cities to demand Morsi's ouster in June 2013, the Obama White House continued to pursue ties with Muslim Brotherhood forces within the Syrian opposition, in Libya, and elsewhere in the Middle East/North Africa (MENA) region.

The Obama Administration, in pursuit of the President's personal commitment to regime change in Damascus, looked to the Syrian Muslim Brotherhood to anchor a post-Bashar Assad government, well after the Morsi disaster had played out in Egypt.

Turkey's ruling AKP Party, another Muslim Brotherhood-allied institution, has enjoyed Obama's enthusiastic support for years, bolstered by the U.S. President's intimate ties to current Turkish President Recep Erdogan. Erdogan and the AKP have been President Obama's closest partners in the Muslim world in the drive to oust Assad.

Dennis Ross Fudges

On Dec. 10, 2015, Ambassador Dennis Ross, who served on President Obama's National Security Council during the first term, was asked a pointed question from *Executive Intelligence Review* about the Obama embrace of the Muslim Brothers. The exchange took place at a public forum, co-sponsored by Marymount Manhattan College and the American Iranian Council (AIC) in New York City.

EIR asked: "In 2010, when you were working at

creative commons/jonathan rashad

Egypt's Muslim Brotherhood President Mohamed Morsi (at the microphone), and Egyptian Muslim Brotherhood's Deputy Supreme Guide Khairat al-Shater (right).

the National Security Council, you worked on implementing Presidential Study Directive 11, dealing with prospects for the coming instability in the Middle East and North Africa. This study began in the late summer of 2010, some months prior to the outbreak of what came to be called the Arab Spring. While the document remains classified, along with Presidential Policy Directive 13, which I understand was the final product from PSD 11, David Ignatius wrote a series of columns on the policy, indicating that President Obama viewed the Muslim Brotherhood as a moderate, possibly progressive force within political Islam, and that the Administration adopted a policy of closer cooperation with the Muslim Brotherhood in Egypt, Libya, Tunisia, and Syria. FOIA documents released in the last two years show that you, along with Gayle Smith, Samantha Power, and Michael McFaul, were the four project coordinators for the PSD 11/PPD 13 work. What can you tell us about that process and the policy that emerged, and how would you view it, in hindsight today?"

Ross, clearly taken aback by the question, went into a long, evasive, roundabout explanation, claiming that the real objective of the Administration policy was to encourage "pluralism" and "reform" in the Middle East. He ultimately admitted that the policy did support working with the Muslim Brotherhood, if it was committed to non-violence and was willing to accept a "pluralist order" in the region; although he denied that PSD 11 or PPD 13 explicitly named the Muslim Brotherhood.

He admitted that there was a clear perception throughout the Middle East region during the height of the so-called Arab Spring, that President Obama had embraced the Muslim Brotherhood and was responsible for the ouster of President Hosni Mubarak. When President Obama hesitated to criticize President Morsi, Ross conceded, the impression that President Obama was "partial to the Muslim Brotherhood" took on a life of its own.

David Ignatius, writing in the *Washington Post* on March 6, 2011, just days after President Obama signed PPD 13, presented a somewhat more honest account of the Obama Administration's schemes for the MENA region. He quoted directly from PSD 11, as well as from Deputy National Security Advisor Ben Rhodes.

Clearly he had been given a White House script and access to at least portions of the classified Presidential Study Directive. Writing under the headline "Obama's

Low-Key Strategy for the Middle East," Ignatius reported that the Administration had quietly put through a dramatic policy change, in response to the events in Tunisia and Egypt, and the beginnings of ferment in Libya. The new Obama policy was to back the revolts against the former U.S.-allied regimes, to insist that the opposition be rapidly brought into the transition, that changes had to occur rapidly, starting with the release of political prisoners from jails, and that presidential elections should be held first parliamentary elections or work on constitutional reforms.

In the Egyptian case, Ignatius reported that the Muslim Brotherhood would be a clear part of the "reform" process, noting that the Brotherhood announced it would only run candidates in a third of the parliamentary districts, and would not run a candidate for president. The Muslim Brotherhood's Freedom and Justice Party broke both of those promises early on.

FOIA Documents Tell Much More

Through an ongoing Freedom of Information Act (FOIA) law suit against the U.S. State Department, *EIR* has learned a great deal more about the Obama Administration's policy shift. All told, 98 emails from a number of White House, NSC and State Department officials between August 2010 and February 2011, detailed the extensive deliberations that went into the response to President Obama's PSD 11. They confirmed that Dennis Ross, Gayle Smith, Samantha Power, and Michael McFaul, all at the time senior staff at the NSC, were in charge of the policy review.

While the Administration has refused, to date, to declassify PSD 11 and PPD 13, a separate segment of the FOIA suit seeking all State Department documents on the Muslim Brotherhood, revealed precisely how pivotal the Brotherhood was to the "new" Obama Administration policy towards the Arab Spring.

A State Department cable dated June 30, 2011 from the Near East Asia Office of Press and Public Diplomacy (NEA/PPD) acknowledged that the U.S. welcomed dialogue with the Muslim Brotherhood, on the basis that they were part of the non-violent and peaceful opposition, and that the organization had a large number of women in their ranks. The document acknowledged that U.S. contact with the Muslim Brotherhood "has occurred on and off since the 1980s." But under the new policy, the document continued, the United States will now be in touch with Muslim Broth-

Mohammed Sawan, head of the Libyan Muslim Brotherhood, and an interlocutor of the Obama Administration.

erhood members who are not elected members of national parliament.

A second cable from the same day reported that Secretary of State Hillary Clinton, while traveling in Budapest, Hungary, took questions from reporters and read from a newly produced State Department fact-sheet on the changed relations with the Muslim Brotherhood. The document stated "There is no U.S. legal prohibition against dealing with the Muslim Brotherhood itself, which long ago renounced violence as a means to achieve political change in Egypt and which is not regarded by Washington as a foreign terrorist organization."

An internal email circulating the same day in the State Department's press office made clear that the question to Secretary Clinton was planted, to allow for the policy change to be announced ("FW: MB-S got the question at her presser today"). The next day, another State Department cable distributed an article from the Turkish daily *Hurriyet:* "*Hurriyet* reports MB spokesperson Muhammad Saad al-Katani said, 'We would be happy to set up such contacts with all, because such ties will lead us to clear our vision.' Signaling the relationship between the MB and the US will grow more over the coming period."

A heavily redacted State Department cable from Embassy Cairo dated March 2, 2012, "Subject: Muslim Brotherhood Businessmen Seek Common Ground with U.S. Investors," detailed a Feb. 19 meeting hosted by U.S. Ambassador to Egypt Anne Patterson with "business and economic leaders from the MB/Freedom & Justice Party and major U.S. investors to foster dialog between the groups."

On April 1, 2012, a 'Sensitive but Unclassified' cable from Tripoli, Libya, reported that the next day, a steering committee member of the Libyan Muslim Brotherhood would be meeting with embassy officials in Benghazi, in preparation for a delegation of Libyan Muslim Brotherhood members traveling to Washington to attend a Carnegie Endowment conference on "Islamists in Power." The cable noted that the Muslim Brotherhood had recently formed a political party, the Justice and Construction Party, and the State Department anticipated "they would likely have strong showing in the upcoming elections, based on strength of its network in Libya, its broad support, and its being a truly national party. 25% of members are women."

Indeed, on April 4, Deputy Secretary of State William Burns met in Washington with members of the Muslim Brotherhood from Libya, Egypt, Tunisia, and other countries in the MENA region. A section of the memo, prepared for the Burns meeting, under "Points to Raise," cited "Commitment to working with Islamists" on the basis of freedom of religion, noting "Islamists that win elections will have to work with liberal parties to write a constitution and govern in an inclusive fashion."

In describing the Carnegie conference, the State Department cable, classified 'Confidential,' noted: "Twelve high-level representatives of and individuals affiliated with Islamist parties from Egypt, Tunisia, Morocco, Jordan, and Libya are attending the conference," and "those from Egypt, Tunisia, Morocco and Jordan + 2 Carnegie officials will come to Dept. for roundtable with Burns 4/4." The remainder of the lengthy document was redacted.

One reason for the attempt to cloak the Muslim Brotherhood visit in semi-secrecy was that a number of the participants were on State Department and Department of Homeland Security (DHS) terrorist watch lists, barring them from entering the United States. In several instances, the State Department got DHS to over-ride the watch lists, and State Department employees met the arriving Muslim Brotherhood delegates at the Customs stations when they arrived for the Carnegie event.

Cable 687 from Embassy Cairo to Secretary of State Clinton, dated May 10, 2012, detailed a presentation by the Egyptian Muslim Brotherhood's Deputy Supreme Guide Khairat al-Shater on May 7 at the American Chamber of Commerce. The State Department report characterized al-Shater as "a highly successful businessman despite 12 years in prison during the Mubarak era," who "remains one of the most influential MB/FJP advisors on economic and business issues." The cable concluded that his speech before the American Chamber of Commerce "reflected the inclusive and pragmatic approach the MB/FJP have sought to present in their effort to ease business and investor fears over an Islamist-led government."

On June 18, Ambassador Patterson sent a 'Classified' cable to Secretary Clinton, reporting that, while votes were still being tallied, the embassy was certain that Mohammed Morsi, the candidate of the Freedom and Justice Party/MB, had won the presidential election.

Two days later, in another 'Classified' cable, Patterson expressed concerns about security for U.S. embassy personnel, based on the widely held view that the United States had backed Morsi's presidential candidacy, and that there was a possibility of vote fraud and a deployment of the Egyptian military onto the streets to block Morsi's victory.

The Obama Administration took a similar approach to the Libyan Muslim Brotherhood, with Deputy Secretary of State Burns meeting on July 14, 2012 with the head of the Libyan Muslim Brotherhood, Mohammed Sawan. The preparatory memorandum, labeled 'Sensitive but Unclassified' (it was subsequently classified 'Confidential' on Jan. 12, 2014, in the midst of the *EIR* FOIA suit), noted that "MB was banned for 3 decades, and returned last year after years in exile in Europe and US, selected new leadership, and began to plan for active role in Libya's political future. Libyan Muslim Brotherhood-affiliated Peace and Construction Party, headed by former political prisoner Sawan, created in 3/12."

A lengthy cable 1098 from Embassy Tripoli to Secretary of State Clinton dated Sept. 11, 2012,—the day Ambassador Christopher Stevens and three other American officials were killed in a pre-planned heavily armed attack on the U.S. mission and a CIA annex in Benghazi,—contained some stunning revelations about the security conditions in the east of Libya. Under a subhead "Militia commanders discuss the Muslim Brotherhood, Jibril, their political aspirations, the economy and security," the memo described a series of talks that Ambassador Stevens had on Sept. 9 with local militia commanders who "discussed the very fluid relationships and blurry lines they say define membership in Benghazi-based brigades under the February 17, Libya Shield, and SSC umbrellas."

The militia leaders claimed to maintain control over the Libyan Armed Forces Chief of Staff Yousef Mangoush, who relied on them to secure eastern Libya, and in return, provided them with weapons, ammunition and other equipment. "Some or all support MB's JCP candidate, Electricity Minister Awad Al Barasi for PM because if elected he'd appoint Feb 17 Brigade Commander Fawza Bukatif as Def Min, which would open Def Ministry and other security ministries to plum-appointments for favored brigade commanders and give Feb 17 and Libya Shield tacit control of armed forces. Criticized US support of NFA leader and PM candidate Jibril."

The memo warned:"If Jibril won, they said, they would not continue to guarantee security in Benghazi, a critical function they asserted they were currently providing." It concluded, "Growing problems in security would discourage foreign investment and lead to stagnation in eastern Libya, but USG could play a role by pressuring US biz to invest in Benghazi."

It would be hours after that cable was transmitted back to Washington that al-Qaeda-affiliated terrorists from Ansar al-Sharia launched their assault on the U.S. compounds. Ansar al-Sharia had a seat on the Public Safety Committee of Benghazi, headed by the very militia officials and Muslim Brotherhood representatives who had threatened Ambassador Stevens just 48 hours earlier.

Still Covering Up Colossal Failure

Even after the Egyptian fiasco of Muslim Brotherhood rule, and the cold blooded murders of Ambassador Stevens and three other American officials in Benghazi, President Obama continued to court the Muslim Brotherhood, particularly in Syria, where they made up a core element of the Islamist forces, armed by Washington to overthrow the Assad government.

To this day, there has been no Administration repudiation of that horribly failed policy,—just more of the same coverup and lies.

Every Day Counts In Today's Showdown To Save Civilization

What Brunelleschi Knew And How He Knew It

This edited transcript of LaRouche PAC's regular "New Paradigm" internet television show of April 9, 2014, now nearly two years old, complements the discussions of the role of Filippo Brunelleschi contained in EIR's *previous issue of Dec 11. It has never before appeared in* EIR.

Megan Beets: Good afternoon, today is April 9th, [2014]. My name is Megan Beets, and I am joined in the studio today by Mr. Lyndon LaRouche and Jason Ross, of the LaRouche PAC Scientific Research Team.

Now, just to set the context of today's discussion, the world is currently suffering the effects of what has been an absolutely fatal breakdown crisis in political guts and political leadership in the United States: We have a fascist President installed in the White House, who is acting on behalf of a British Empire to drive the world to the brink of thermonuclear war, a war of extinction. Now, in the United States, three-quarters or more of the American people, no matter your so-called party affiliation, hate this guy, want him out—need him out for their survival.

Now, what is the so-called "opposition" party, the Republican Party in the Congress, doing? What is their strategy? Well, rather than act to impeach this guy, and he *is* impeachable, their strategy is... "We'll wait for the next election. We'll wait until 2016, when we'll install Jeb Bush" or something like that.". . . .

Now, not only are we responsible for stopping the threat of thermonuclear war, but those of us who are willing to take leadership, such as yourself, Mr. LaRouche, are also leading the fight to ensure the basis for the continuation of civilization. And this is what we're going to get into today: What is the basis for the operation of the human species in the universe? What is the basis for human progress, and progress of mankind on Earth, and beyond?

As you have outlined recently, what people have to understand are two crucial groupings of scientists in the past 600 years of mankind's history: The later grouping, which we covered a couple of weeks ago, being the current of Gauss and Riemann into Planck, Einstein and

creative commons/Amada44

Brunelleschi's Dome, Santa Maria del Fiore, Florence, Italy.

Vernadsky; that was set up on the basis of the earlier grouping which Jason's going to discuss today, which is, Filippo Brunelleschi, Cusa, and Kepler. So with that, I'll turn it over to you.

Who was Brunelleschi?

Jason Ross: All right. Yes, as we discussed last week and then three weeks ago on these triads, and just to reference a couple of other things for people to check out, besides those shows of March 19th and April 2nd, are also Mr. LaRouche's two recent papers, "Is Satan Still Operating from Inside Bertrand Russell's Corpse?" and "The Incompetence of Twentieth Century Science Education."

So, today we are going to go into some more detail on the first triad, that of Brunelleschi, Cusa, and Kepler, in particular on Brunelleschi. Just to read a quote from you, Mr. LaRouche, from the show of March 19th:

Okay, so let's look at these two cases: All right, what did Brunelleschi prove? Brunelleschi proved the falseness of the straight line, of the existence of the straight line in the small. That was his great achievement. He extrapolated from the understanding that you can not use arbitrary predetermined lines in any way, to determine how processes work.

And then a little later, you said:

He came up with a whole new architecture, but more: He took the simple thing of a simple, hanging chain, the hanging chain model. ... Then came Kepler as a follower, implicitly of Brunelleschi, and specifically of Cusa; he was very explicit about it. He solved the problem. So a third member of the triad came up with a solution! But Kepler's solution depended upon both the implications of what Brunelleschi had done, which enabled Cusa to make his discovery. But the solution was not yet reached. The solution was done by Kepler.

You added:

So all competent modern science depends upon the reference to Kepler, in terms of Brunelleschi and Cusa. Anyone who eliminates any one of these three, Brunelleschi, Cusa, or Kepler, all as

one group, is an incompetent in science, intrinsically.

So, to make sure we are not incompetents in science, we're today going to focus on Brunelleschi, about whom I was mostly unaware until rather recently, so we have some things to share about him.

Obviously, the most pronounced achievement of Brunelleschi is the dome of the Cathedral of Florence, the Cathedral of Santa Maria del Fiore. This is still today the largest masonry dome in existence on Earth, although it was built centuries ago. The cathedral was actually begun in 1296, which was when the first stone was laid, and some of the initial layout of the length of the church was designed. In part of the building boom of the Fourteenth Century of Florence, continued work was done, and then there was a debate, and actually a referendum, in 1367, to choose on the general design of the cathedral. The two choices were between the designs of one Neri di Fioravanti and Giovanni di Lapo Ghini.

The two designs differed in that Giovanni di Lapo Ghini proposed a Gothic style cathedral, one where,— unlike the dome as it looks today,—it doesn't have the flying buttresses, which are the stone arches on the outside of the cathedral that help hold it inwards, that you see in the Gothic cathedrals; those buttresses allowed the walls to have many more windows that let in a lot of light, and that was why they were built. That was one of the two proposals. The other one, from Neri di Fioravanti, did not go with a lot of large windows as you can see, but got rid of all those buttresses, going for a simpler look, what he thought was a more "Florentine" look.

And the referendum was held and this is the design that won: Brunelleschi's father had actually voted in the referendum, and he had voted for this design, so there's a family connection to it. Part of the proposal from 1367 was for a dome of this sort to be built.

Now, nobody knew how to build that dome in 1367, but they still boldly decided that was the design they would pursue, and they would build up the rest of the cathedral and worry about how to build the dome later, which is what ended up happening. So the cathedral was being built; Brunelleschi was born in 1377. He lived a couple of blocks away from the cathedral, so as a young child, as a young man, he would have been familiar with the construction work that was taking place. Everyone in Florence knew this was going on, and he was right next to it.

FIGURE 1

creative commons/sailko

Depictions of the Sacrifice of Isaac, done for the competition to adorn the doors of the Baptistry next to Santa Maria del Fiore. On the left, the panel by Lorenzo Ghiberti; on the right, that by Brunelleschi.

FIGURE 2

*Masaccio's The Holy Trinity (*Santa Trinità), *a fresco in Santa Maria Novella in Florence.*

So, Brunelleschi became apprenticed as a goldsmith, which at the time was among the highest of the trades, because of the detailed work that was done, and because of the things that you could do as a goldsmith. Brunelleschi—we don't have the actual model, but supposedly he even worked on building a clock that was powered by springs rather than weights, in his work as a goldsmith, which, if true, would have been the first spring-powered clock. It's a little bit uncertain, as is much about his life.

His Early Breakthroughs

So the cathedral's being built. The plan, to give a sense of the proportions, I'm not sure if you can see, but there are people standing at the very top, on the lantern, at the railing there, and you can see how tiny they are compared to the size of this dome. The peak of that cross above the gold ball at the top, is 375 feet in the air. So this is significantly taller than the U.S. Capitol—this is a tremendous building.

So, back to Brunelleschi's life: In 1401 or 1402, there's a competition that he entered to design doors for the Baptistery of Florence, and he's one of two finalists in this competition, along with Lorenzo Ghiberti. So, I would actually encourage everybody to look at these— it's hard to see these in this video, I know; but if you take a closer look at them, you can compare the designs of Ghiberti on the left, and Brunelleschi on the right. (**Figure 1**), This was one sample panel of Abraham's sacrifice of Isaac, before the angel stops him. Ghiberti won; Brunelleschi was not commissioned to build the doors, and he then set off on a trip to Rome. He went to Rome with his friend, Donatello, where he studied buildings, he studied construction, he studied art, to the extent that there were things to look at.

And in doing this, he developed the concept of perspective. So Brunelleschi really made a breakthrough in how vision works, and how perspective works, and made the breakthrough out of the flat paintings, that were seen, to the actually spatial ones.

This is a painting by his student Masaccio. (**Figure 2**) It's called *The Trinity* and it's in Florence. This was

FIGURE 3

FIGURE 4

The Pantheon in Rome, completed in approximately 126 A.D. by the Emperor Hadrian.

The Roman aqueduct Pont du Gard, *opened in 60 A.D. in the south of France.*

the first real perspective painting. And you can see, as you look at it, you've got Christ; you've got above him a dove, which is the Holy Spirit; and then you have God the Father behind him. And you can tell that there's a sense of depth, you can tell by the way that ceiling is drawn behind him that it really appears that this goes back in space. And you can imagine when it was first painted,—and the paint wasn't falling apart as it is now,—how realistic this must have looked, and what a shock it was to people to see a wall that looks as if it actually extends back.

Today, we might take this for granted, but it wasn't always known. And this came from Brunelleschi. Leon Battista Alberti, who later wrote a book on painting, credited Brunelleschi as the inventor of perspective, which in this painting uses a vanishing point to create a real three-dimensional space, such that you can recreate the scene as a three-dimensional model, and you can place Christ and the Father,—you can actually place them spatially. This turns something flat into something spatial.

So, among the things that Brunelleschi would have seen in Rome was the Pantheon. (**Figure 3**) Now the Pantheon, built by Emperor Hadrian—a Roman temple to all of the gods,—is almost exactly the same width as the Dome of the Cathedral in Florence. They're basically the same width. The Pantheon, however, is a purely circular dome, whereas the one in Florence, as we saw, had ribs, and it's in the shape of an octagon.

Now, even though this is the same width, it's not as tall as Florence's Cathedral, and if you look at it from the side, you can barely even tell that there's a dome. In fact, it's ugly from the outside; it's hardly an inspiring sight. But this gave Brunelleschi an opportunity to look at how the construction occurred.

In the Pantheon, for example, the walls at the base of the dome are twenty-three feet thick: That's how thick it had to be made to contain all of the stress, the architects thought. Also, when this dome was built, it was built by putting up a huge amount of scaffolding that actually filled up the entire space of the dome, upon which the concrete was then set, and then hardened, and then the wood was all removed.

This use of wood to set the shape is called "centering," and let's take a look at why that would be done. This is a Roman aqueduct; this is the Pont du Gard, today in France. (**Figure 4**) And so, if you want to make a structure that's wider than the longest piece of stone that you can make, you have to put many pieces of stone together, and the arch is the shape that lets you span a distance. These arches were made with centering: If you just started building the blocks from the side, they'd of course just fall in. It's only once you have the entire arch built and put in the keystone, that it then supports itself; before that it's not stable, it doesn't have an internal stability. And we'll turn to what Brunelleschi did on this.

So this is a picture of some more modern—well, more contemporary—arch-building in Morocco, (**Figure 5**) and you can see there's the centering, which is put underneath the arch: It sets the shape; you then lay the bricks. Once the mortar hardens, you can then remove the centering, and the arch maintains itself.

FIGURE 5

FIGURE 6

creative common/Haven La Chance

Arch-building in Morocco in September 2011.

Iranian Historical Photographic Gallery

The Taq Kasra arch, located in Salman Pak, Iraq. It is estimated to have been erected in the now-disappeared city of Ctesiphon in approximately 540 A.D.

Here's another, very old, large arch: This is a vault in what is today Iraq. (**Figure 6**) This was built 1500 years ago in one of the Persian empires, and this is in the shape of an upside-down catenary. Catenary means "chain," it comes from the word for chain: If you hang a chain—I meant to have one but I forgot—but if you have a chain or rope, and you let it hang, it'll make a shape which is this, upside-down. It's a very stable shape.

His Challenge to Stupidity

Let's return to the Dome: The year is 1418, it's August, and a competition is again being held in Florence. Brunelleschi has returned; this is 50 years after the 1367 referendum that decided on the overall shape. The Cathedral is built, and they're ready to figure out how to start building the Dome. And just as in the doors of the Baptistery, again, the final two designers are Ghiberti and Brunelleschi. Brunelleschi, in proposing how to build this Dome, says he's going to do it without any centering, he's not going to use any scaffolding: He's going to build this Dome, piece by piece, such that it's stable as it's being constructed, not only when it's finished.

Nobody else thought this was possible. This really astonished people. The way the story goes, is that when people said, "how're you going to build it? How're you going to build it?," he gave them a challenge: he said, "I'll tell you how. To figure it out, you have to figure out how to make an egg stand stably on its end."

So he challenged them; people tried, and they couldn't do it. And they said, "All right, Brunelleschi,

how do *you* make an egg stand on its end?" And he said, "like this"—he cracked the bottom of the egg, so it was flat, and then set the egg there. And as the story goes, "Well, if we knew that, we all could have done it!"

And he said, "Exactly! But you didn't know that." He said, "I know how to build this Dome. You wouldn't understand it. I'm your man. Hire me."

Well, the decision wasn't reached until 1420, but he was hired—along with Ghiberti, which was sort of awkward, but Brunelleschi was in charge of the construction, and so in 1420 he was able to start the building of it.

Now, while the committee was still deciding who would build the Dome, how it would be done, Brunelleschi got a few other commissions, so I want to show some pictures of some of his other work: This is the Ospedale degli Innocenti, which was an orphanage. (**Figure 7**) And in the likeness of the great palaces of the rich families, Brunelleschi built what's called a *loggia*, this patio or this porch on the front of it. This is something he had designed; he really changed the way the columns were used, and this was part of an overall humanist orientation of concern for human beings: a large, beautiful building, built at the expense of one of the guilds, to take care of the orphan children of the city.

This is another work of his, and—out of order,—this is the Pazzi Chapel, the "singing chapel," which actually came much more towards the end of his life. (**Figure 8**)

Now, back to the Dome: Just to give a sense of how high this thing is, the Cathedral reaches up to a height of 140 feet,—that's the height of the whole length of the nave; then you see the Dome. Before it starts, there's another section, which has those large circular windows—it's called the "tambour,"—that's another 30 feet. So, the Dome begins at 170 feet! That's already more than double the height at which the Pantheon's dome began in Rome. It then extends up to a height of over 300 feet, more than double, again, the height of the Pantheon.

FIGURE 7

The façade of the Ospedale degli Innocenti, *Florence.*

Now, in terms of why centering couldn't be done, you couldn't get enough wood to build this. It would have taken between 500 and 1,000 trees; there were no trees that were even tall enough. In later centuries, the only place the British Navy could get timber for their masts of over 100 feet for its largest ships, was in the New World. There simply weren't enough tall trees anywhere in Europe that they could find. And the same was true at the time this was built. It would just be impossible.

The other thing is that because of the time it took the masonry to set,—because it ended up taking sixteen years to build this Dome,—if a wood frame had been built, it would have lost its shape over sixteen years, and it wouldn't have worked anyway! So, even if you had had all the wood, you couldn't have done this with a center.

Inventions

But Brunelleschi had a totally different approach to space and to the physical nature of construction. Instead of looking at a shape very geometrically, as was done with the earlier arches and domes we saw, where you design a geometric shape that you'd like,—It's not inherently stable during its construction, so you have to support it,—get the shape, and then you're fine,—Brunelleschi has built a structure—obviously, he succeeded—where along the way, it's stable. So the stability is built into every part of the Dome, not into the Dome as a whole. As an early Italian historian had said, "It was as if every part of the Dome was the keystone" that

gave the stability: It was everywhere stable.

Now, let's talk about actually building the Dome and the techniques that Brunelleschi used. One of them was that there's a lot of material that you've got to bring up there. If you were going to have workmen carry four million bricks up those steps, it's going to take you forever, and it just wouldn't work. So what Brunelleschi had done: he designed a new kind of winch. (**Figure 9**) Before Brunelleschi, everybody used treadmills for building these cathedrals,—like the hamster wheel you see at the pet store, but a large one, with people in it. And people would run in these treadmills, and it would twist and wind a rope, which would lift up along a

FIGURE 8

creative commons/Gryffindor

Brunelleschi's Pazzi Chapel, completed in 1443.

FIGURE 9

Brunelleschi's winch, featuring forward and reverse gears.

FIGURE 10

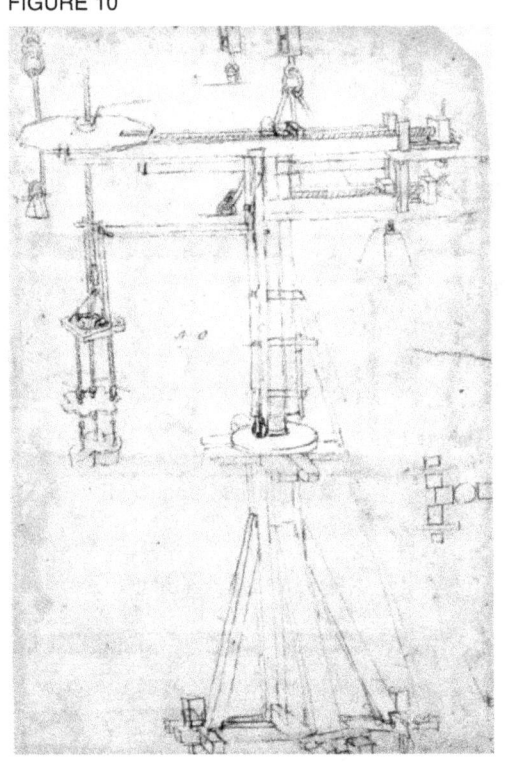

Code Ambrosiano

Leonardo da Vinci's depiction of Brunelleschi's crane.

pulley, it would lift a load up to the top, where you would have your materials delivered.

Well, instead of having people do this job, Brunelleschi's design used oxen—this illustration uses a horse instead,—that instead of walking in a treadmill, they walked in a circle. And he also developed for the first time, a gear system. So just like in your car, you can switch your car into reverse,—the same thing with this. You could see the axle that's being twisted by the animals, this vertical axle. There's two different ways it can engage with the horizontal winch system. And by raising or lowering the axle that the animals are turning, you can put it in either forward or reverse, because every time you bring a bucket of materials up, you obviously have to bring it back down again.

Apparently oxen are very stubborn, and they will happily walk forward as long as you ask them to, but they won't walk backwards. So to avoid having to get them out of their harnesses, and turn them around, Brunelleschi developed this transmission system so they could always be oxen, and walk forward, and everybody was happy.

Another thing that he had to do, was once you got the material up the top of the Dome, you had to then put it in the right place. Some of these things that he used, weighed thousands of tons. We're going to get to what

some of these large components were. So he also designed a crane, which is perhaps somewhat hard to see, but a crane, called a "castello." (**Figure 10**) This is a drawing by da Vinci—da Vinci was actually involved later with the work on the Cathedral. Da Vinci sketched a number of the things that Brunelleschi had done, and so some people thought that he had invented them. but he was just drawing what Brunelleschi had made: a crane complete with counter-weight, so you could position and get all of your larger objects exactly where they needed to be in the Cathedral—another major innovation.

Now, on the shape of it: This is a diagram of the shape of the Dome. (**Figure 11**) It's not a spherical dome. It goes up to a higher level, so it's called a "pointed fifth," where you take two portions of a circle, and then they would meet at a point, except there's a hole left at the center of the Dome, and this is part of

FIGURE 11

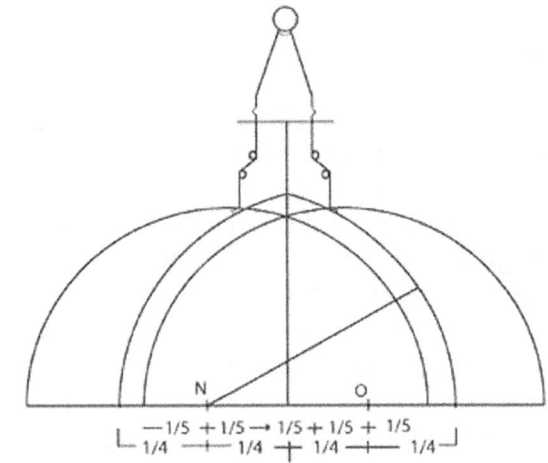

Lando Bartoli

Drawings adapted from Bartoli's Requiem per una cupola, *Florence, 1988.*

FIGURE 12

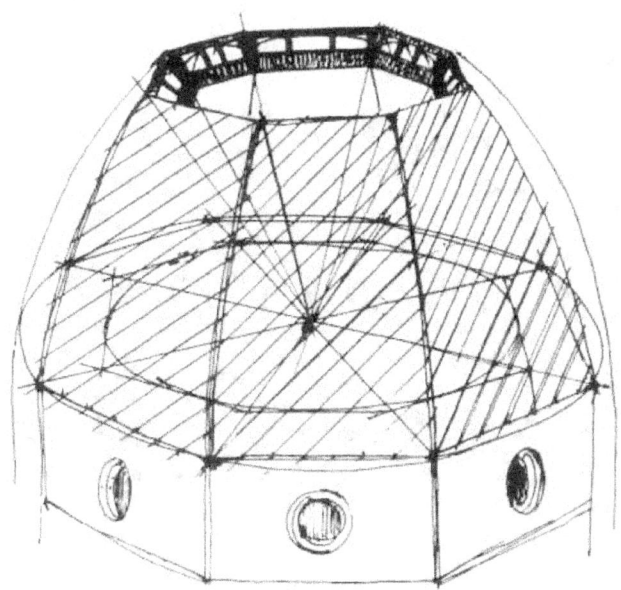

THE BRICKLAYING APPARATUS

Bartoli's perspective sketch of the brick-laying apparatus, set up like an inverted pyramid with a single center of convergence. The diagonal lines across each rib show the spiral path of the herringbone brick work

(a) Side view

Height of the parallel X tangent to the corner of the vault cell.

Rise

Height of the projection of the rise of the parallel arc comprehended between two edges (belly of the catenary).

(b) Top view

Lando Bartoli

Drawings adapted from Bartoli's Requiem per una cupola, *Florence, 1988.*

what made it so tall and magnificent compared with the frankly ugly Pantheon. It also reduces the amount of horizontal stress at the base by designing it this way.

So, when Brunelleschi did his construction—this shows you—the Dome is actually two domes: there an inner dome, and then there is an outer dome which is the one we see from the outside. (**Figure 12**) The inner dome, at its base—remember the Pantheon in Rome, twenty-three feet thick; Brunelleschi's inner dome is only seven feet thick at the base and only five feet thick at the apex. The outer dome is only *two feet thick* at the base, and *one foot thick* at the top. Imagine, something of this size, that outer dome, only *one foot thick*: The outer dome is supported by the inner dome.

So in doing this, he had to use this catenary again, and he actually built *catenas*, he built chains inside the Dome, like the hoops in a barrel that hold the staves together. So this is a picture of one of them. (**Figure 13**) There are four sandstone chains, where large blocks of sandstone had been quarried: These are

some of the things you needed the crane for, because people couldn't have carried these and put them into place. They're just too heavy. The crane would be used.

Enemies Attack Him

So these sandstone chains were built, in not exactly circles, because the thing's octagonal, but there are four of these chains that help hold the stress in, that pull the Cathedral inward so it doesn't explode outwards. The records also indicate that there are four iron chains as well, although they can't be seen. If they're there,

FIGURE 13

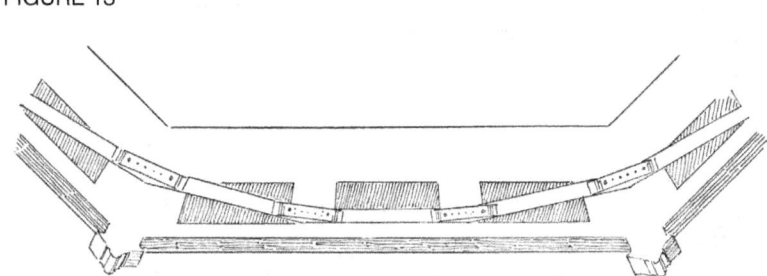

One of the four sandstone chains still visible in the Dome.

they're inside the masonry; and also a wooden chain, which is still there—a wooden chain to help hold the stress, which is astonishing.

Another aspect of the construction—well, let's go ahead and do this: Some of the bricks that were laid in the Dome, which was made out of brick rather than stone—brick is lighter than stone, because it has so many air pockets in it. He had the workmen lay the bricks in a very unusual pattern, and it also required unusually shaped bricks, custom-made, custom-shaped bricks: four million bricks.

To get a sense of the work involved, these bricks, after they were formed and put in their molds—it might take two years of preparation before they would be fired,—seasoning time—and the unique pattern that Brunelleschi used, this herringbone or fishbone pattern, meant that you didn't have just pure shelves of bricks all the same, that could then shear apart. (**Figure 14**) It also meant that, because of the orientation, it helped the lower levels support the ones above it. So every aspect of this is unique in terms of the engineering, the industrial engineering to produce everything, in terms of the actual construction techniques.

Okay, a couple more things about the construction: Brunelleschi also received the world's first patent. It didn't work out so well, but he built a ship to bring the marble from the quarries to Florence. As you see, the ribs on the Dome are a nice white color; that's from marble which had then been placed around the brick. And Brunelleschi said, "I'll make a ship that'll do this," and some people think it was to have been powered by either treadmills or oxen that would actually have paddlewheels. Unfortunately the ship sank, the marble was lost; some of it was recovered in an amazing salvage operation. But this just shows you how many different things Brunelleschi's working on: perspective, construction, engineering.

One other thing about the construction is that, according to the official records, only one workman died in building this Dome, which is phenomenal, considering the height. Brunelleschi had safety rules, safety harnesses, safety platforms. The people working at the very highest levels weren't allowed to drink wine, pure wine—they had to dilute their wine with one-third water, so they wouldn't be quite so drunk while working at those heights. And there were strict rules that no one was allowed to sit in the baskets when they were going up and down; you had to use the steps.

As he was building this Dome, at a certain point, Brunelleschi was thrown in jail for not paying his dues to the guild, which was a very small amount of money, and was obviously a political attack against him. And he was attacked explicitly by some of his detractors. People were more cultured at this time, and when they insulted each other, on occasion, they wrote sonnets. So, I'd like to read you these shared insult sonnets. This is from an acquaintance of Ghiberti who attacked Brunelleschi, and he wrote this sonnet to him!

> O you deep fountain, pit of ignorance,
> You miserable beast and imbecile,
> Who thinks uncertain things can be made visible:
> There is no substance to your alchemy.
> The fickle mob, eternally deceived
> In all its hope, may still believe you,
> But never will you, worthless nobody,
> Make that come true which is impossible.
> So if the "Badalon," your water bird,
> Were ever finished—which can never be—
> I would no longer read on Dante at school
> But finish my existence with my hand.
> Because I am certain that you are mad, as you
>   hardly know
> Your own profession. Leave us, please, alone.

FIGURE 14

The herringbone brickwork in the space between the inner and outer domes.

So this guy didn't have to commit suicide, as he had offered, because Brunelleschi's ship, the "Badalon," didn't work. But here's Brunelleschi's response.

When hope is given to us by Heaven,
O you ridiculous-looking beast,
We rise above corruptible matter
And gain the strength of clearest sight.
A fool will lose what hope he has,
For all experience disappoints him.
For wise men nothing that exists
Remains unseen; they do not share
The idle dreams of would-be scholars.
Only the artist, not the fool
Discovers that which nature hides.
Therefore untangle the web of your verses,
Lest they strike sour notes in the dance
When your "impossible" comes to pass.

Columbus and Kepler

So, it's very blatant: What you're doing is impossible, and you're an ignorant beast, so give up, it'll never happen, "experience teaches us it's impossible..." And look at what Brunelleschi said, "Untangle the web of your verses, lest they strike sour notes in the dance, when your 'impossible' comes to pass."

So, a few more things about the Dome: The cupola was completed in 1436, which was a momentous year. Pope Eugene IV came to consecrate the Cathedral. The bishop laid the last brick in the cupola later that year. And then, from 1439 for several years, the Council of Florence—which would have been the Council of Ferrara except that the plague had them move to Florence, courtesy of some financial help from the Medicis—the Council of Florence, organized by Cusa, was held in this amazing Cathedral, the cupola of which had just been completed. And there's no doubt that the experience of such an awesome work helped the conference, gave a new impetus and concept to the Council. I'm not going to say too much more about that: We need to have a whole discussion about Cusa, but that's not happening right now.

So, the last few parts: In 1446, Brunelleschi passes away, after having seen the cupola finished. And then, as I said, some other people are involved, as I said. Da Vinci as one of the workmen in Verrocchio's workshop helped cast the large bronze ball that you see at the top; and then in 1474, or '75, Toscanelli added a plate into

FIGURE 15

The Renaissance astonomical instrument called the gnomon in the Cathedral of Santa Maria del Fiore, invented in 1475 by Paolo Toscanelli, and restored by Father Leonardo Ximenes in 1754.

the lantern with a hole in it, so that the Sun would make a nice spot down below. (**Figure 15**) He used this to correct the Alfonsine astronomical tables, to have the most accurate observations of the Sun that had ever yet been made. Due to the incredible height of the Dome and its stability, it was now possible to have greater precision than ever before by watching—basically, it's a sundial—the spot move along floor. That marbled circle that you see there is the summer solstice.

So, Toscanelli was able to redesign these tables which were used by navigators to get around the seas. He works on a world map; Toscanelli had written to the Portuguese royal court to propose sailing west to get to China. He didn't hear back from them, but later Christopher Columbus found Toscanelli's letter, and wrote back to him, very excited. So Toscanelli and Columbus, in 1481, entered into a correspondence about this; in 1486, Columbus petitioned to have an audience with the court of Spain, Ferdinand and Isabella. And as we know, in 1492, armed with the knowledge of astronomy from Toscanelli, and a map provided him by Toscanelli, he set sail west to reach the Orient.

So the Dome, in a very real way, helped in the creation of the New World. I know that's a lot already, but I do want to say a little bit about Kepler, too.

Just very briefly, on this triad—and Cusa, we're going to have to come back to—but what Brunelleschi had done with understanding that in the small, space isn't geometric, it's physical,—this is what Kepler used to solve a problem that had been puzzling him since he was a young man in college. It was in astronomy: Why do the planets move the way that they do,— not just individually, but all of them? Why does the Solar System move as it does, and he did think it was a *Solar* System.

In his first major book, from 1596, the *Mysterium Cosmographicum*, Kepler published this model (**Figure 16**) for the distances between the various planets in the Solar System; Kepler said that they wouldn't just have arbitrary distances, there must be some reason to it. So what he did was that he looked at something that was characteristic of space itself, which was these five Platonic solids, as they're known. They get small toward the center, but you can see that we have spheres, separated by a cube; inside it we see the triangle-based tetrahedron; inside it a dodecahedron; and then an icosahedron, and an octahedron.

Those five shapes are the only ways that you can divide up a sphere evenly, with regular shapes. In other words, it's the only five ways that you could, for example, take an orange, and cut up the peel into tiles, such that all the tiles look exactly the same and were regular shapes—only five of them.

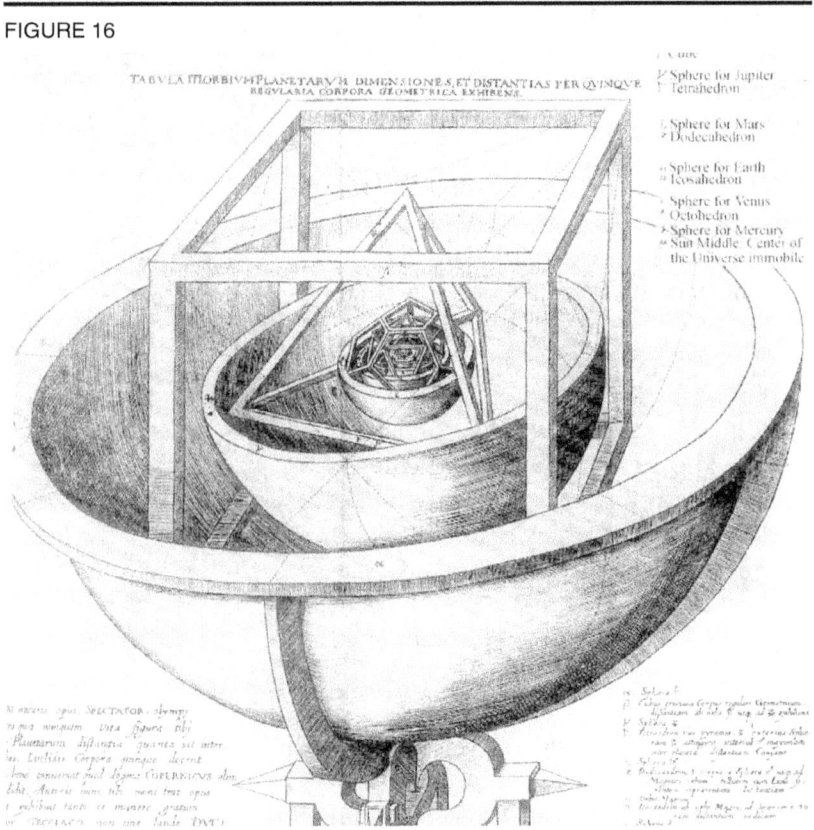

FIGURE 16

From Kepler's Mysterium Cosmographicum.

From Brunelleschi to Kepler

Why are there only five? Space seems to be empty: It doesn't seem to have any characteristics about it, but if you look at doing things in space, you find that some actions are possible, and some aren't. So Kepler believed that given that these were something inherent in how space works, that it would then be found in the spatial organization of planets.

To determine whether he was right or not, he had to get a more accurate idea about how the planets moved, so in his second very major work, *The New Astronomy* he completely revolutionized the process of astronomy: very briefly, he took this Brunelleschi approach, that in the small, there is no linearity; there is only physical action. And he implemented his idea that he had had since his college days,—that the Sun was making the planets move,—and developed the idea that at each moment, the distance from the Sun was determining how much the Sun was moving the planet and would determine its speed. He then had to figure out a way to use that motion at each moment, and turn it into an orbit as a whole.

He also had to come back to the distances of the planets, because these solids indicate overall one distance for each planet, but every planet has two characteristic distances—its closest distance from the Sun and its farthest distance. To figure this out, Kepler then moved to another domain—it seems like another; it seems like another sensory domain,—even though he goes beyond the senses,—namely sound.

So just as these solids divide the spatial space, Kepler also looked at dividing aural, "heard" space, the space of hearing, of sound, of music. And by looking at the harmonic intervals, not by building up music from the half-step, from the smallest musical interval—he did not do that! Instead, he looked at the larger ones that were most stable: the octave, the fifth, for example. He built up an idea of how to create the scale, and then looked at how the planets could achieve a musical completeness: How could the planets move, such that they created both the major and the minor scales? (**Figure 17**)

So Kepler puts himself in God's shoes; he designs the Solar System himself; he explains why he would have first used the solids as his main grounding, and then he would have incorporated the necessities of music to develop an entirety of the system where noth-

FIGURE 17

MAJOR SCALE

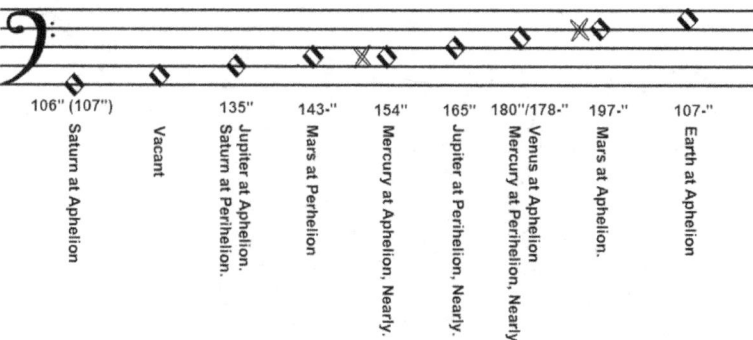

106" (107")		135"	143-"	154"	165"	180"/178-"	197-"	107-"
Saturn at Aphelion	Vacant	Jupiter at Aphelion. Saturn at Perihelion.	Mars at Perihelion	Mercury at Aphelion, Nearly.	Jupiter at Perihelion, Nearly.	Venus at Aphelion Mercury at Perihelion, Nearly.	Mars at Aphelion.	Earth at Aphelion

One of Kepler's depictions in the Harmonia Mundi.

ing was left to chance in the planets, at least not in those two extreme distances. And just to show you,—you don't have to look at the numbers,—but either the closest or farthest motions of the planets had speeds which, if the speed of motion were heard by the Sun,—which doesn't have much of a sense of hearing,—as sounds, then these visual speeds as sounds would be harmonic. What a confluence of different senses that seem to be different! They weren't: It was all one type of harmonics for Kepler.

So putting the whole thing together, Kepler created the Solar System, as a system. He implemented in the small, as Brunelleschi had done, how everything is physical in the small, and he developed the concept of an "all" and why the "all" should be as it is.

We'll talk more later in other shows about Cusa, who obviously we just mentioned here, as well as the other triad: about Planck in the small, Einstein in the large, the paradoxes between them, and how to resolve that. But hopefully, we provided some good insight into why—how it is that these three, Brunelleschi, Cusa, and Kepler, helped define modern science, and why we have to know what they did.

Lyndon LaRouche: Well, first of all, one thing which is left out here, is the question of the catenary. Because you have two concepts which are at the center of Brunelleschi's work: one is the infinitesimal, and it was always,—this was the understanding of light. The attempt to understand a system of light, which was one of his earlier works. The second was the hanging chain principle.

Now, the hanging chain principle is something which destroys entirely the concept of linear space and

time. His whole design, his construction, was based on the hanging chain principle, which existed widely in Italy. You had these deep clefts and so forth, and you would have bridges from one side of cleft to the other side, and you would walk across these bridges, the bridges would dance, [laughter] themselves. And this is the famous song....

Ross: Oh, "Funiculi, funicula."

The Struggle against Zeus

LaRouche: Yes, that was the song which was on this theme of the hanging chain. So what happened, is now suddenly you are out of the area of space as such, entirely; it does not exist. What exists is action in space, and you have to define the action in space by its own characteristic. And the hanging chain principle is a demonstration of that characteristic.

So this is the relationship—you know, from that point on, everything that was the so-called "Classical Greek," heretofore Classical Greek, fell apart. Because there was no way you could have a linear construction of the universe. And through the whole process, that's what you're getting at: there's no linear construction order of the universe. It is not based on a mathematical system.

So mathematics is the deadening of the soul, and we see the mathematicians, we see they have Dead Souls. It's like the accountants: The accountants have the characteristics of having Dead Souls. They die in the middle of their work, but they weren't going anyplace anyway.

So this is what the crucial issue is. So the idea, the notion that there is an infinitesimal, comes not from the small. It comes from the large, because we experience the relatively large. And we find that the principle of action does not correspond to a linear extrapolation. And then, you get everything which then comes from Kepler's work, is actually a finished work! Which is why I've defined this thing as a finished work. That Kepler made a phased completion of a concept, of the idea of *physical space*, action in physical space, as opposed to linear space. So the point is, it was everything against Euclid, and everything that Euclid represented was recognized as being *evil*. And the necessity was to find a principle which corresponded to that which is not evil.

And evil was equated with slavery: raw human behavior, as a slavery, or a system which reduced itself to slavery. It comes up in the case of the Great Pyramids, where the lie was the attempt to interpret the Great Pyramids as being a linear construction, made by slaves and so forth—nonsense! It couldn't have been done that way. They were floating these things down the Nile, and that's why it was there,—they were floating these things. They were using sand as a fluid, and they were using the sand as a fluid form, as a means of construction.

And at the base of these Great Pyramids, what you had there were not slave quarters,—these were engineering quarters! So the Great Pyramid project was an engineering project which used the Nile and used the sands of the desert—it was not as much desert then, but the sands of the desert were used as a device, an engineering device. By moving sand and moving water and displacing one thing and another, you came up with an engineering scheme. And what they called the "slave quarters" in the standard interpretation were actually the engineering headquarters, in which the families lived in these quarters, next to these pyramidal constructions. They lived there, and they did the work.

But they did the work based on use of sand and water as media of action. It's a completely different conception!

So the struggle has always been the anti-Zeusian struggle. Zeusians always insisted that you could do things only one way, by massive use of slaves: the human being as a slave, with no constructive, no dynamic conception whatsoever. And so what the history was, was based on this fraud, this assumption that you have to start from slaves, from primitive human work, done primitively.

The idea of the intellect, the development of the intellect, was completely opposed. And so what you get in this when you get to the hanging chain principle,—you see a very simple demonstration by these hanging chain bridges particularly characteristic of Italy—"Funiculi, Funicula"—that this kind of process was a characteristic, a physical characteristic of physical space-time. It wasn't the whole characteristic, but it was a reflection of the characteristic.

egyptphoto.ncf.ca

The pyramids at Giza, Egypt: great projects which were completed in 2540 B.C.

So, he didn't go to zero, the concept of a mathematical zero point. There was never a zero point in his work! The point was, the universe was defined by an *action process*, a process of action, which is only cognizable by the noëtic powers of humanity; that is, the use of the hanging chain as a bridge across a chasm, was typical of this kind of demonstration.

So the problem has been to get away from what has happened essentially since the year 1900, the beginning of the century. This was a return to primitivism! It was actually a force of evil! And don't kid yourself about this thing: These guys were all evil. Their motives were evil. David Hilbert was not a simple-minded character in Paris in 1900: This guy was an evil guy! He was motivated by evil! He produced garbage, which is what evil generally does.

Ross: It's sort of unavoidable.

LaRouche: Yes, it is. But the point is, we're still stuck with people who think in terms of a Euclidean system, and Euclideans are stupid, they're inherently stupid. They're chronically stupid.

Gauss and Riemann

Ross: Right. You know, the fight in science, in reality it's a fight against this oligarchical concept; it's a fight against the axioms that are wrong, that prevent you from seeing things that are true. But there are contemporary people who try to say that they are scientists and talk about what science is: They present it as though the only polemic they have to make is against some fundamentalist evangelical, who believes that the Bible is a textbook,—so they say: "Well, science is about the fact that we use experiments to know what's true, and not just assumptions."

Well, that's kind of obvious, but where do you develop the new ideas? How do you break through axioms that blind you to things? And that is the real key to science. But if you look at what happened in 1900, with Hilbert's proposal and then Russell taking it up with relish, and saying that we are going to systematize thinking,—creativity became not breaking apart the underlying axioms; it became finding an unexpected, but deducible theorem. Creativity became finding a new formula to them. That's what they turned science into: "Follow the facts, what's the formula?"

LaRouche: Well, you have two things, you have first of all,—it was Cusa who actually gave us Leibniz. And it was through that process that this happened. So you had a definition of science with the work of Cusa, and then what Kepler proved, with the nature of physical space and time, eliminated all linear conceptions of the organization of space and time. Now, Leibniz thus represented the most typical of this kind of questioning insight, based on this understanding, exploration of this understanding, which became modern science.

But then we went to another phase, and the new phase actually came at the beginning of the next century, essentially. And then you had this evolution in process, a great tumultuous evolution, which came especially with Gauss. And then Gauss gives you, as a result, directly: the real heir of Gauss is Riemann.

I mean, the visual connection of these two is wonderful: Here's Riemann, who's a real student of the work of Gauss, actually. And Gauss is sitting, aged, in his last years of life, and he's sitting there, without reported facial expression, but sitting there, and here is his student saying everything, telling all the secrets of Gauss in his great Habilitation Dissertation,—especially the initial critique which defines that, rips everything apart! He rips them all apart, just simply, in about three paragraphs; he tears everything apart—with one statement.

You can imagine what Gauss's reaction is.

Then you get this final paragraph, which horrifies all

these people: "And now, we must leave the department of mathematics, for physics…" [laughs] And that! That's the declaration which is Gauss's secret all this time! Not to explain to people *how* he had done things, but give them a finished example of how it works. All his work, like on the question of the organization of physical space, and so forth—he's hiding things! All the time, he's ducking. He says, well, I will give you an explanation of how this worked.

The Reversal in 1900

Ross: He's hiding his mind. And that's—like Riemann. One way you could look at it, is he's saying, the mind is real, the mind exists.

LaRouche: Well, then you could go through a whole group of people, from the end of that century into the beginning of the Twentieth Century, and you find a real florescence of creativity, coming in various parts of Europe and elsewhere, and also in the United States to some degree. An idea of space and time, and man's relationship in space and time,—what you get especially with Hamilton.

And most people today are incapable of understanding Hamilton. Which, of course, I'm making a big issue of. If you don't understand Hamilton's work, you're an idiot. If you think you know what the Constitution of the United States is, you're an idiot, and you don't know what it's all about anyway. Franklin understood it; he understood it in his way.

So this is the issue. So, we're stuck with people whose work is to make them stupid, which is what our school systems do. They make people stupid: By teaching Euclid. If you teach Euclid as a basis of education, going from primary into secondary school education, you are going to destroy the intellectual capabilities of nearly all of those students. I know: I went through it.

I didn't even know what Euclid was at that point, but I knew it was wrong. So I just said what it was. And you should have seen the howling and screaming that went on from that point, for three years! About me, about this issue and similar issues. The point is, they were all brainwashed. The whole school—it was considered a very good school, just north of Boston. You had two secondary schools which were notable at that point. One was the so-called classical school, and the other was the engineering school and so forth. And you had people in there who really had some ability to think. But they were polluted on this question of geometry.

Ross: It was like a monopoly: It's hard to think about physical geometry without thinking of— "Oh, you mean, Euclid?" "No— constructive geometry doesn't equal Euclid."

LaRouche: Well, that's the whole point. And so the point is, we still have the problem that most people today, most university professors for example, in sciences, are crippled. I had the biggest problem with the Fusion Energy Foundation. We had one real genius in there, who was the leader of the whole operation; a *real* genius.

Ross: Yes, Robert Moon.

LaRouche: Yes. But the others were secondary: They all had talents, developed talents, which they had acquired in the university, but unfortunately they had also been through a secondary school education, and the secondary school education had destroyed their ability to go higher. They would be able, by working with experimental approaches, to conduct specific kinds of experiments which would work, and they would make new discoveries of specific kinds of experiments which could work.

But their idea of the progress of science was entirely based on mathematics. And you saw this particularly in my age, you can imagine what has happened from 1900, from the beginning of the Twentieth Century: The Twentieth Century was the degeneration. Everything from Cusa and so forth up, was in a direction of progress. It was a fight for progress. And the fight for progress continued.

But with the 1900, with this change, and especially what happened after the end of World War I, where the German community was destroyed, and where this was done explicitly. Since that time there has been a degeneration in the educational system of universities and schools. And that's the big problem I have politically: I have people, very bright people out there, some of them. *But!* they all are soft on Bertrand Russell. And Bertrand Russell is the equivalent of the incarnate virtue of Satan.

Beets: Well, you've pointed out many times in your

The Greek mathematician Euclid, who worked in the Egyptian Emperor Ptolemy's Alexandria court circa 300 B.C.

fights within the Fusion Energy Foundation, that it always came up around the issue of Kepler versus Newton, and that you got these very insightful scientists who would go into fits of insanity over the idea that *Newton* was the real scientist, whereas Kepler did something or other, and now we have these formulas called Kepler's laws.

But in effect, what Kepler did was revolutionize science, the same way you're referring to Riemann. Where Riemann said, "Now we leave the domain of mathematics for physics," Kepler had done that: Kepler had taken the discoveries on the basis that was put down by especially Cusa, and he had put that into practice and proven that there is no such thing as a validity of a mathematical or a geometrical language. It's physical: And what has access to the physical is the human mind.

Our Incompetent Scientists

LaRouche: The most important figure after that, is actually Leibniz. Leibniz was the one who made the real breakthrough in defining what the bullshit was. And therefore, the attack on Leibniz—you know, you have also this spectacle: Leibniz is not yet dead, and they're waiting for his death before they dare go ahead into the next step—and that's what happened. That's what happened to science! They're waiting for Leibniz to die, because he was the genius who had made what Kepler had done understandable. And made it a principle.

And therefore, the educational system from that point on, from the Eighteenth Century on, the educational system was degenerating. And the minds of people were degenerating. They could make progress in specific qualified areas, but they were still using mathematics! And the one thing that you would learn from the Renaissance, was that mathematics is *not* the principle on which physics is based!

Ross: Ironically, a lot of people will say that Newton is the beginning of physics.

LaRouche: He was the death of it!

Ross: Right, yeah.

Isaac Newton (1643-1727) shown in a panic, as his writings on alchemy are burning in 1693. Legend has it "the dog did it."

Beets: And Leibniz showed very efficiently in his correspondence with Newton's proxy, Dr. Samuel Clarke, that the belief in fixed mathematics and the belief that space and time are linear and empty,—which is the mathematical description,—he ends up showing that that's Satanic. That the root of that is actually Satanism, which is exactly what is reincarnated in Bertrand Russell.

LaRouche: Exactly. And Bertrand Russell was very aware of that. That that's what it is, and that's what we're dealing with today. That's what our whole organization is dealing with, essentially, to the extent it functions at all: You're fighting against these fixed standards, where people who came out of colleges and so forth,—they may have been bright, and so forth, but they still had this attachment to what they had been trained to believe, and tried to explain everything in terms of what they had been trained to believe. And the minute they would click on that, "Well, this is what we had been trained to believe," this becomes the affirmation for them of what is truthfulness!

And that's one of our biggest problems we have with our best, leading people, politically. They're not competent! Because they have, underneath them, they have assumptions, presumptions which are false. And it's like belief in Satan; you know, no matter how smart you are, you still believe in Satan, and therefore, there's something wrong with you.

Ross: Yes. I feel as if I know what you're getting at. For me, it's really resonating with the concept of the ontological versus the methodological transfinite in your economics book, *So, You Wish To Learn All About Economics?* Because there, you had contrasted those who would still accept that there is something transfinite, or transcendental about the mind, as a method, that there are people who might say, "Yes, the mind does something that's inexplicable. But the things that it discovers should be deducible from the axioms." Versus, the true—what you called in that book the ontological transfinite,—where the way the mind works is itself reflecting something about how the universe works: that there is a coherence between them; that the *mind itself* is a part of nature.

And there's this bizarre idea that it shouldn't be. You know, that's what Gauss had to do. He had the way he thought, he had his mind, he had the way his creativity worked. But then he presented things as though he hadn't found them that way. So it can be kind of irritating to read his work, because you know he's not telling you how he came up with something!

LaRouche: If you look at his earlier mathematical works, you see it.

Ross: Yeah! In his proof of the Fundamental Theorem of Algebra, then he has a lot of raucous fun; he's polemical, he's attacking people, he does it very explicitly—well, almost explicitly,—tell you how he's thinking.

LaRouche: Until he gets to a certain point, and then he's told, "Take it easy, buddy." And thereafter, he would not explain his experimental discoveries. He would describe them. And then Riemann changed that! Riemann, with the Habilitation Dissertation, just destroyed this whole thing! It's there. You can go through it, read that; it's the most up-to-date thing you can imagine today when you're getting into a classroom. You bring Riemann into a classroom, a mathematics, physics classroom, academic level, even postgraduate level—you get a real freakout!

Ross: They say, "Go to the physics department, get outta here. You're spoiling our fun." [laughter]

LaRouche: Well, the point is, "We don't believe in shitting on our food."

Russell's Evil Doctrine

Ross: Their idea of fun is maybe not the best.

LaRouche: It's essentially that!

Beets: What you're bringing up,—this is the crucial issue we face today, because this is an oligarchical prison cell that people are willfully putting themselves in. And by clinging to the idea that the human mind does not actually have a consequence in the physical universe, that all we know and all we do is a derivative of mathematics and deduction and experience, we're submitting to what is an oligarchical system, an extinction system. Because if we don't break out of that, and if we don't return to a truly human policy structure, which is these breakthroughs in principle of human mind, implemented in a physical economic system which has been best embodied by the American System of economics,—we are facing extinction.

LaRouche: And the phenomenon is, we're dealing with a population whose standard of veracity is clinically insane. Because they believe in things that are not true. They're living in a fantasy world, where there's no understanding whatsoever of the truth of things—because *they don't want to be ostracized*! And the principle of ostracism is the key instrument of making people stupid. Tell them, "Don't do that, you'll be ostracized! Nobody will talk to you; if you start talking like that, people are going to wonder if something is wrong with you."

You say, "No, there's nothing wrong with me,—there's a lot wrong with you. But maybe your case is hopeless. Is that possible?" It's the only way you can respond to them. "I mean, you may believe that, but maybe it's just because you're insane. Or, maybe just stupid."

They don't like that—I don't know why. Giving them valid information on which their future existence may depend! But they don't like it... too bad!

So what you do, is you work in the process of history which creates points of contradiction. And you exploit the contradictory evidence to shatter the evil presumptions. You're seeing that now. You're on the edge of exactly that: that what's happening from Asia, which relative to the trans-Atlantic region, is predominantly sane. It may be imperfect, highly imperfect, but it's different!

Asia is progressing, and in the trans-Atlantic region, you have a disease called the green disease. And the green disease is pure evil! And people who believe in it will behave like evil people: They will attack viciously those who do not accept the green philosophy. But every green person is an idiot! Every person who's green should be thrown out of any department of sci-

ence, in secondary schools and also higher... they're intrinsically incompetent, they are fraudulent. Their premises are wrong, have no correspondence to reality. They believe in mathematics, and mathematics has inherently no truth to it.

They believe in language in the ordinary sense, and there's no truth in language in an ordinary sense, just as Riemann says in his final paragraph of his Habilitation Dissertation: We must now leave the department of mathematics, for physics.

And that's exactly what the reaction, was against in the famous events in Paris in 1900. That's exactly what Hilbert was doing: he was setting up a counterposition to science—in mathematics! And then you had this evil Russell, who went out as a real fanatic, to spread this doctrine of evil. It was based on the British Empire, the power of the British Empire to enforce it. And World War II and the things that led into it were actually this process of *destruction of the human mind*.

And the transition from the process of—well, it actually comes from Bismarck, Bismarck's [1890] ouster was the turning point. And you have this whole series of wars and so forth which were breaking out at that point, because they recognized that the victory of Abraham Lincoln, who they assassinated as a result, had been an affirmation of the American Revolution. So he was assassinated! Just the same way that John F. Kennedy was assassinated, that his brother was assassinated. The assassination attempt against Ronald Reagan was part of the same series as the assassination of Kennedy and his brother.

Coming Breakthroughs in Science

And Reagan was a little bit tough physically; because of his whole background, he was a very physical guy. So he survived the assassination attack against him. But he was crippled and pretty much put out of action for a while in recovering from that assassination attack, and the Bushes moved in.

So what happens is, that Reagan actually comes in as the escape from the Democratic Party's stupidity of the whole thing,—the stupidity that occurred in the entirety of the 1970s. It was an era of stupidity.

And the attempted assassination of him, which didn't work out as an assassination, but it was surely an assassination attack,—was to bring in the Bushes! If he had died, there would have been a Bush Administration all the way through! And we would have had the Bush

NASA/JPL-Caltec

Man in the Solar System: A hazard avoidance camera on the rover Curiosity in one of its maneuvers over Mars.

problem then, already. Which we have now with what was done against Bill Clinton. And Bill was not prepared to deal with the shock that they were throwing at him. That was his weakness. He had also a Vice President who was better at vice than anything else. And that was not helpful.

So that's where we are! We're in a point where there are certain standards which we can know, and which you can find by tracing the history of science and history of culture the same way. You can find a track which is consistent. And you find out early, with what happened with Vernadsky's work,—how Vernadsky has made another breakthrough—he's dead now, but he's made a breakthrough which is a new conception of mankind in the universe.

Because for the first time, human life—not life as such, but human life, becomes a standard of understanding of the whole Solar System and beyond. Because it's man *in* the Solar System, which is now the standard of truth, of relative truth. It's the best we can

do right now, so far. And that's why the space issue is so urgently important. We have to get beyond what Vernadsky actually achieved in the transition to the concept of life as primary, human life as primary. And that's what was happening at the turn of the Twentieth Century! And that's what they tried to head off!

And that's what the fight is now. That's what our fight is. We have now entered into a new space of history. We're now going into space; that is, we *have* to go into space, we have no way of escaping that responsibility. Which means we have to redefine everything we think in terms of just everything that's happening on Earth. It's not just happening on Earth! The threats to mankind's existence immediately beyond Earth, or affecting Earth from beyond, are the real issues. And the point is to understand mankind and understand what the human mind actually represents, from the standpoint of looking into the future, looking into—the idea, are we going to Mars? We're stupid!

Obviously, you can't live on Mars! No one yet has the capability to actually live on Mars. Or to live on asteroids. Human beings don't have that capability. A very short time, with highly specialized preconditions and followup, and then their life is at risk also, because of the effects of the little bit of strain they have. But we can put machines out there. We can put processes in action out there; we can control them from Earth; we can set up institutions that function, controlled from Earth, in nearby space, on the Moon, and beyond.

Mankind then begins to control nearby space. And that's what we must, among other things, do! Because we're going to have to change the condition of Earth; we're going to see what we can do about influencing the Sun. These are the kinds of things which are the future.

And you have minds like those of the Renaissance, those minds, and the Renaissance tradition that came out of that, until it was crushed! That's the reality. It's the only thing worth studying.

Beets: And it's the fulfillment of what Kepler did. Kepler subsumed the observed bodies of the planets out there into a single Solar System, under the principle of mind. And we have to fulfill that by subsuming the Solar System by the principle of the human mind.

LaRouche: Exactly! Precisely! This is precisely it! And people have got to get out of their smallness. And these cases,—like these cases of the Renaissance,—are a crucial point in the history of mankind. And it remains still the crucial issue for mankind, to understand what that principle is. It's the most important thing we can do.

Because this system is not going to work! It can not work. It is inherently a failure; there's no way you can civilize it; you have to change it for something better.

Ross: Into a different, totally new idea of the future. The Renaissance proved for sure that we can go way beyond what we had done in the past. That venerating antiquity was not the way to go. The future could go far beyond that, and the same thing today. You have to have a vision of the future that goes far beyond where we are today.

LaRouche: And not to recognize the fallacies of sense-perception, and to understand them: that's where our problem lies. Because when you get into the Renaissance, you get a turning point in all of human history. It's a precious turning point which is specific to that particular century. And what comes with Kepler's discovery, when Kepler defines the principle of the Solar system,—which is an ontological conception, not a formal one,—that conception changes everything! And people who don't accept that change are inherently stupid, and a threat to civilization. It's true!

Because it's like the guy who drives off the cliff, saying, "I have my rights." Pfff, boom! They're not so smart, you know.

Beets: I've noticed.

LaRouche: That's why this is so important: to get into the ontological implications of these issues, is what the issue is! Not the effect. Contrary to *Die Hauptsache ist der Effekt* ["The main thing is the effect"], it is not just effect! *Die Hauptsache* insists, there is something better. The future is the effect.

Beets: Okay, that's a good place to leave it for this week.

Don't Believe the Popular Lies!

Dec. 10—Corrupt popular opinion and media insist that Obama's removal is impossible. Indeed, they go so far as to try to insist that it isn't even being discussed. But thanks first of all, and most of all to the key catalytic role of Lyndon LaRouche's "Manhattan Project,"— neither assertion is true. In fact, there is active discussion of the need for Obama's removal at the highest levels of government. No more lying: it can be done, it must be done, and we must see to it that it is done, and done quickly.

Sometimes an action which appears ostensibly local to a single place, like the "Manhattan Project," has universal effect: think of Brunelleschi's cupola in Florence, for example.

Part of what these corrupt media and popular opinion are hiding from you, is that there is now an active bill before Congress, which lists eleven offenses which would trigger impeachment proceedings against any President who committed any of them. The most prominent of these offenses are precisely the "high crimes and misdemeanors" for which Lyndon LaRouche has indicted Barack Obama in his weekly dialogues with the Manhattan Project.

Congressman Ted Yoho (R-Fla.) introduced H. Res 198 on April 13 of this year. It is short and sweet. After a few "whereases," its operative section simply says the following:

The House of Representatives declares the following Presidential actions shall constitute impeachable "high crimes and misdemeanors" within the meaning of Article II, section 4, which will cause the House to vote an article or articles of impeachment to send to the Senate for trial—

(1) initiating war without express congressional authorization;

(2) killing American citizens in the United States or abroad who are not then engaged in active hostilities against the United States without due process (unless the killing was necessary to prevent imminent serious physical danger to third parties);

(3) failing to superintend subordinates guilty of chronic constitutional abuses;

(4) spending appropriated funds in violation of conditions imposed for expenditure;

To Prevent a Nuclear Armageddon

Dec. 13—In Theodore Andromidas's article in the *EIR* of September 25, 2015 , he proves conclusively that the underlying necessity for passage of the 25th Amendment was that an impaired President would have the power to start a nuclear war, or would be unable to meet such a challenge if it were instigated by another nation. He documents that in the case of Richard Nixon, during the end phase of the Watergate proceedings, James Schlesinger, then Defense Secretary, had ordered the Chairman of the Joint Chiefs of Staff not to take any orders from Nixon. Article 4 of the 25th Amendment was his authority to do so. Schlesinger's was a pre-emptive measure, in case Nixon had gotten it into his head to start something irrevocable.

At Obama's instigation, with British-Saudi backing, Turkish President Erdogan ordered a Turkish F-16 to ambush a Russian Su-24 tactical bomber whose coordinates were given to Turkey by the United States. It was indeed an act of war against an ally in the fight against ISIS. Obama is insane all right,—but in the way that Hitler was insane.

We have to face reality and move now.

(5) intentionally lying to Congress to obtain an authorization for war;

(6) failing to take care that the laws be faithfully executed through signing statements or systematic policies of nonenforcement;

(7) substituting executive agreements for treaties;

(8) intentionally lying under oath to a Federal judge or grand jury;

(9) misusing Federal agencies to advance a partisan political agenda;

(10) refusing to comply with a congressional subpoena for documents or testimony issued for a legitimate legislative purpose; and

(11) issuing Executive orders or Presidential memoranda that infringe upon or circumvent the constitutional powers of Congress.

Note that Rep. Yoho's bill will come into effect as soon as it is passed by a majority of the House of Representatives. There is no need for any action by the Senate. Rep. Yoho has two cosponsors: Republicans Jeff Duncan of South Carolina and Tom McClintock of California.

Republican Justin Amash of Michigan was a cosponsor, but withdrew on June 9. We don't yet know his reasons for withdrawing, but they probably involve the intensity of the struggle,—in a fight which some would have you believe is not even happening at all.

All the focus now on the immediate need to remove Obama, has led some to look again at the provisions of Section 4 of the 25th Amendment to the U.S. Constitution, which prescribes how to remove a President "who is unable to discharge the powers and duties of his office," but who fails to step down of his own accord,—requiring a little shove, one might say.

The usual presentation of Section 4,—indeed what has been our usual presentation of Section 4,—says that the Vice President and a majority of cabinet members must vote to declare the President's (in this case) mental incapacity. But in fact, that is not what it says. That is but one alternative. The other alternative is that the Houses of Congress establish by law another "body," which would be in effect a special commission to investigate and vote on the President's capacity to continue in office.

Quite a difference, potentially.